TRUCK ACCIDENTS KILL

How the trucking industry has
created a killing field on US roads and
what we can do to stop the carnage

BY BRAD PISTOTNIK
TRUCK ACCIDENT LAWYER

ISBN: 1502753928
ISBN 13: 9781502753922
Library of Congress Control Number: 2014918104
CreateSpace Independent Publishing Platform
North Charleston, South Carolina

DEDICATION

First and foremost, this book is dedicated to my wife, Christina, and my daughter, JoAnna. This book would not be here without their love and support, and without the hard work of my staff. It is also dedicated to the truck accident victims and their families who inspired this work. They not only provided the vital background and information needed to pursue their claims, but also are responsible for the depth of understanding and compassion I gained during my time as their lawyer. Although I secured substantial financial compensation for those victims and their families, the money paled in comparison to the pain they suffered and the losses they endured. No amount of money can justify such loss, and, for this reason, this book is truly for the truck accident victims and their families.

INTRODUCTION

A T ANY TIME, day or night, one would be hard-pressed to travel an American interstate highway, drive for more than a minute or two, and not see an eighteen-wheel tractor-trailer truck on the same highway. With an outdated rail system and many landlocked states, big rigs and other commercial trucks play a huge role in moving goods across the USA. These large trucks number in the millions and often share the overcrowded highways with millions more cars and other vehicles. Often, this mixture of cars and trucks creates traffic flow problems that cause traffic congestion and thousands of accidents. This book informs the reader how large trucks and commercial vehicles become involved in many accidents that cause catastrophic human injuries, death, and suffering due to negligent truck drivers and truck companies' failure to abide by safety rules.

Many drivers become intimidated when passing or being passed by one of these big-rig trucks, and rightfully so. Most eighteen-wheel trucks are far larger and sturdier than anything else they share the road with. If drivers knew that many truck drivers are fatigued, overworked, and pushed to the limit to deliver their loads on a tight deadline, regardless of safety regulations, they would likely be afraid to come near a big rig. The chances of being involved in an accident with a tractor-trailer truck are far higher than most of us realize. Large trucks and fatigued drivers are a well-documented major contributor to accidents that lead to tragic and life-altering results for the victims and their families.

There are many statistics that relate to truck accidents. This book provides an analysis of a great deal of the statistics related to driver fatigue, poor maintenance, and failure to comply with government safety regulations. The statistics should be very alarming to the drivers of other vehicles that share the road with large commercial trucks. Large trucks make up approximately 4 percent of the registered vehicles on the nation's roadways, but they account for almost 10 percent of the nation's accidents that involve fatalities.

Truck crashes continue to increase every year, along with the number of injuries and fatalities that are associated with these crashes. A lackadaisical effort by motor carriers to properly train their drivers in defensive-driving techniques and safety training is a contributing factor. This disregard for safety compliance is one reason why victims of truck accidents should retain competent truck accident attorneys.

Why do truck drivers of so-called eighteen-wheelers, big rigs, tractor-trailers, or whatever you choose to call them have to be better trained than other drivers on the road? We know that the probability of injury and death is much greater in accidents that involve large commercial trucks. The trucks' high profile makes them more prone to rollover accidents and more susceptible to weather elements, such as high winds. The weight of these big rigs requires a much longer stopping distance than that of cars and small trucks. Professional truck drivers bear a huge responsibility to drive their big rigs with the utmost of care in light of the horrific consequences that may result if they don't. A higher standard of care is essential. The motor carriers are more concerned with deadlines and moving cargo rapidly for pay by mile or by weight. These payment incentives favor profits over public safety and are too often the cause behind vehicular fatalities.

Truck Accidents Kill is an authoritative text meant for professionals in the areas of motor-carrier safety, truck accident litigation, risk management, and regulatory fields. This book is written to enable safety-conscious individuals in our society who care about safety improvements to the motor-carrier industry to have a better understanding of what can be done to prevent accidents involving large trucks. This book attempts to provide a basic understanding of the Federal Motor Carrier Safety Regulations (FMCSR) as they apply to safety considerations associated with truck drivers and motor carriers.

My main goal in writing this book is to show truck accident lawyers how to prepare for trial and successfully litigate a case against a trucking or insurance company. Property damage, injuries, and death are the typical harms that are litigated in a trucking accident. This book will teach you how to attack the defendants from every angle and how to maximize the case value when preparing for trial and litigation. Every conceivable avenue for an attack is discussed and studied to increase the compensation and the case's settlement value.

I fully expect my clients to recover for their losses and damages, such as extreme medical bills, loss of the ability to work and provide for their families, immeasurable human pain and suffering, disability, and other horrific life changes.

This book includes a statistical description and analysis of certain factors that affect safety as it relates to the general motoring public and its contact with large trucks, tractor-trailers, and commercial motor vehicles. The present amount of accidents that result in severe injuries and death is unacceptable. Regulations can be increased. Regulatory compliance can be increased. Insurance coverage for the entire motor carrier industry needs to be reevaluated and increased to meet an acceptable level of mandatory minimum limits of coverage to protect the general motoring public.

Certain thoughts and opinions are expressed in this book that are solely devoted to the improvement of public safety on the intrastate highways. With the continuing growth of the motor carrier and transportation industry, accidents, injuries, and deaths continue to increase at a startling rate. It is hoped that the thoughts expressed within this book will aid and assist those persons in society who have a desire to see safety improved for the motoring public.

Some of the chapters of this book are written to assist trial attorneys in the presentation of regulatory evidence so that those individuals who have been killed, injured, and had their lives catastrophically changed will have advocates with a thorough understanding of the law as it relates to the motor carrier and trucking industry. If one life can be saved, this book has achieved its purpose.

BACKGROUND AND C.V. FOR BRADLEY A. PISTOTNIK

B RADLEY PISTOTNIK HAS been practicing law since 1981. He has litigated against nursing homes across the country, insurance carriers such as Allstate, motor carriers throughout the United States, including Tyson Foods, Archer Daniels Midland (ADM), Federal Express, UPS, and more.

His practice has focused on personal injury cases with severe and catastrophic injuries, such as death, paralysis, coma, amputation, and other physical injuries. His legal work concentrates on accidents involving tractor-trailer trucks and other commercial vehicles, automobiles, and motorcycles, as well as construction site accidents, catastrophic medical malpractice, nursing home negligence, and other cases requiring intensive, skilled litigation.

Attorney Pistotnik graduated from Kansas State University in 1978 with a Bachelor of Science Degree in Business Administration with a major in Marketing. He also graduated from the University of Kansas School of Law and received a Juris Doctorate degree in 1981. He is licensed to practice in Kansas and Oklahoma state courts, and is admitted to practice in the Federal District Court in Kansas. Mr. Pistotnik works frequently in other states, where he is admitted Pro Hac Vice with local counsel, and in that capacity, has represented clients in Illinois, New Mexico, Virginia, Missouri, Texas, and other states.

Attorney Pistotnik is a member of the Board of Governors of the Kansas Association for Justice and the Top 100 Trial Lawyers through the American Trial Lawyers Association. He is also recognized by the American Society of Legal Advocates as a top 100 litigation lawyer.

Attorney Pistotnik has authored articles on the law in the area of tractor-trailer accidents and the Federal Motor Carrier Safety Administration regulations (FMCSR) of the Department of Transportation. Mr. Pistotnik has been a speaker at seminars for the Kansas Bar Association in the area of tractor-trailer accidents. He authored, *Divorce War, 50 Strategies Every Woman Needs to Know to Win* (Adams Media). Mr. Pistotnik appeared on the television show *Geraldo* to talk about his book and accomplishments and has been quoted by the *New York Times* in regard to the Michael Jackson case. He is also an accomplished trial lawyer with numerous verdicts and multimillion dollar settlements.

Attorney Pistotnik currently practices as an accident attorney at Bradley Pistotnik Law, P.A. The firm is located at 10111 E. 21st Street North, Suite 204, Wichita, Kansas 67206. He can be reached at 1-800-241-BRAD or 1-800-241-2723, 316-684-4400, or on his direct mobile line at 316-706-5020. His email is Brad@BradPistotniklaw.com.

He is a member of the following associations:
- American Association for Justice
- American Trial Lawyers Association
- Kansas Bar Association
- Kansas Association for Justice
- Oklahoma Bar Association
- Wichita Bar Association
- American Society of Legal Advocates

TABLE OF CONTENTS

1

TRUCK ACCIDENT FACTORS

VEHICULAR ACCIDENTS ARE the most crucial causes of lifetime injuries, and in many cases fatalities, in the United States. Hundreds of accidents occur every day. A majority of these accidents cause injuries ranging from minor to devastatingly serious, and thousands of families are affected every year. The consequences of these accidents are bound to multiply in magnitude when the vehicle involved is a truck—especially big-rigs, also known as tractor-trailers or eighteen-wheelers. Accidents that occur with commercial trucks are generally far more catastrophic than those involving other vehicles.

The trucking industry in the United States is massive. In 2011, it generated $603.9 billion in gross weight, which represented 80.9 percent of the total freight bill in the United States. According to the American Trucking Association, trucks are responsible for moving 67 percent of the country's freight requirements. A huge number of companies are involved in the US trucking industry. It is estimated that as of December 2010, the total number of for-hire carriers was 408,782, with private carriers totaling an astounding 662,544, and various others totaling 168,680. In 2013, the trucking industry used a massive 523 billion gallons of diesel fuel. A commercial truck at full load is an incredible eighty thousand pounds. In comparison, the average weight of a passenger vehicle is 2,500 to 3,000 pounds. Commercial trucks are massive in terms of capacity, and you can only imagine the amount of damage they cause. The large weight and bulkiness of these commercial trucks restrict the process of turning and moving the truck. This makes them difficult to drive. Even the slightest error on the driver's part can cause the truck to lose balance and control and can result in a devastating accident.

One type of accident that occurs with trucks is an underride accident, where a vehicle slides beneath a large tractor-trailer. The consequences of these accidents are far more damaging and dreadful than are depicted in fast-paced Hollywood action movies. There is no doubt that truck drivers are trained to be far more cautious while driving than the average passenger car driver, but the massive loads and size of the trucks cause accidents every day on the roads. Sadly, it would be almost impossible to eliminate truck accidents, so one must always drive with the utmost caution.

A major contributing factor of truck accidents is the condition of the roads in the United States. If you have had the opportunity to drive across America or even if you have traveled beyond a few state lines, you must have noticed the worsening conditions of the roads. In 1919, a convoy was commissioned by the War Department to travel from the East Coast to the West Coast to build roads. As of today, the Interstate Highway System has laid 42,795 miles of roads all over the country. These roads were not built to last forever. The roads today in the United States have cracks, potholes, and are in rough condition.

Initially, the road network was excellent for cars because trains transported most freight. The railroads performed this job to the best of its ability but the time consumed by it proved unaffordable. This is where the trucks came in, as many companies quickly acknowledged that the interstate was a faster option. With the introduction of trucks on roads, companies had more control over the timing of the deliveries, and they could provide prompt deliveries. However, the road planners failed to predict the importance of trucking as a mode of shipping and thus the damage perpetrated by trucks on American roads was quick.

The creation of potholes is a slow and gradual process. Water finds a place underneath the asphalt when the roads are not adequately sealed and settles into the small spaces between the pavement and the material that is used for the base of roads. The compact water pocket gets pushed down as trucks drive over the roads and, since the water has no other place to go, due to the gravity exerted on it, the water goes deep down and the dirt is forced out in this manner. This process creates a large space beneath the pavement and with the passage of time, the air/water pocket gradually depletes the top layers of the roads and they begin to crack, eventually causing bigger and bigger holes.

Building roads is a complex process as the balance between the initial construction cost and the continued maintenance of the roads has to be considered. For this particular reason, roads should be constructed with a concrete foundation. This would help reduce highway accidents by reducing maintenance costs and eliminating cracks, holes, and defects in the roadway surfaces. Only then would roads not require hefty maintenance. If roads were given a solid foundation, the cracking of the surface would occur less frequently. However, in order to construct such durable roads, a large amount of money would have to be invested initially.

Engineers who plan for the construction of roads have the responsibility of predicting exactly how much the roads will be used and for what purpose. This prediction is difficult, especially for areas where the population and manufacturing facilities are growing. In those areas, the amount of vehicles increases and the load being carried on the roads rises, which increases the cost of maintenance and decreases the life of the roads. It is important to keep the growing needs of people and vehicles in mind when constructing roads and to consider the types of vehicles, especially heavyweight vehicles, that may be using the roadways.

Other contributing factors of truck accidents are driver issues. Those may include drug and alcohol use while driving, carelessness, and fatigue and exhaustion caused by long hours of driving. The general public that shares the roads with commercial trucks is largely not aware of the needs of such large trucks, such as no-zones, off-tracks, and the stopping distances required by such large vehicles. This lack of information can contribute to collisions between trucks and other vehicles. Many large trucks carry hazardous materials. When these trucks are involved in accidents, the danger to the traveling public is increased because of the dangers of volatile and hazardous materials being expelled.

The US federal laws and regulations known as the Federal Motor Carrier Safety Regulations (FMCSR), which are administered by the Department of Transportation (DOT), along with its adjunct administrative agency, the Federal Motor Carrier Safety Administration (FMCSA), were developed to prevent truck drivers from operating over interstate and intrastate highways for more than a certain number of hours per day and per week. The regulations issued under 49 C.F.R. §§ 380 through 399, which are enforceable pursuant to the Motor Carrier Act, PL 96–296, 1980 S 2245, and PL 96–296, July 1, 1980, 94 Stat 793.49 C.F.R. § 390.3(e)(1) & (2), provide that every driver and employee shall be instructed with regard to and shall comply with all applicable regulations contained in the FMCSR. Regulation 49 C.F.R. § 390.5 provides that "motor carrier" means a for-hire motor carrier or a private motor carrier. That term includes a motor carrier's agents, officers, and representatives, as well as employees responsible for hiring, supervising, training, assigning, or dispatching of drivers. Regulation 49 U.S.C. § 14704(a)(2) provides that, "A carrier... is liable for damages sustained by a person as a result of an action or omission of that carrier...in violation of this part."

Regulation 49 U.S.C. § 14101(a) provides that, "A motor carrier shall provide safe and adequate service, equipment and facilities." The FMSCRs are located at 49 C.F.R. § 380 *et seq.* The FMCSRs and the MCA, specifically under the section 49 C.F.R. § 391.1(a) and (b) state, "(a) The rules in this part establish **minimum qualifications** for persons who drive commercial motor vehicles, as, for, or on behalf of motor carriers. The rules in this part **also establish minimum duties of motor carriers with respect to the qualifications of drivers.** (b) A motor carrier who employs himself/herself as a driver must comply with both the rules in this part that apply to motor carriers and the rules in this part that apply to drivers." Regulation 49 C.F.R. § 390.11 imposes duties on the motor carrier to follow the minimum duties and industry minimum standard of care required by the FMCSR and states, "Whenever in part 325 of subchapter A or in this subchapter a duty is prescribed for a driver or a prohibition is imposed upon the driver, it shall be the duty of the motor carrier to require observance of such duty or prohibition. If the motor carrier is a driver, the driver shall likewise be bound."

Many motor carriers violate the minimum duties and standards of care set forth under 49 CFR § 395.8 by failing to adequately document the driver's record of duty status. They violate the minimum duties and standards of care set forth under 49 CFR §§ 395.1–395.3 by requiring drivers to work in excess of the maximum hours and days allowed by federal laws and regulations. They violate the regulations under 49 C.F.R. § 392.3 by requiring drivers to operate a commercial motor vehicle while the driver's ability or alertness is so impaired, or so likely to become impaired through fatigue, illness, or any other cause, as to make it unsafe for him/her to begin or continue to operate the commercial motor vehicle.

Motor carriers sometimes fail to set up adequate safety systems, which then causes their drivers to operate on time deadlines that do not adhere to the hours-of-service regulations. They violate the minimum duties and standards of care set forth under 49 CFR § 383.113 by failing to have adequate safety management controls in place that would require and provide that drivers have the skills required under this regulation.

More importantly, they violate these minimum duties and industry standards of care as set forth under 49 CFR § 391.11 and 391.23 by failing to properly qualify the driver, failing to obtain the federally required information on the application for employment of the driver, which requires an investigation of the driver's safety performance history with the DOT-regulated employers during the preceding three years and that further requires the prospective motor carrier to investigate, at a minimum, the information listed in this paragraph from all previous employers of the applicant.

Another significant problem with the motor carrier exists where they violate the minimum duties and industry standards of care set forth under 49 CFR § 391.31 by failing to properly road test their drivers. This regulation requires that a person shall not drive a commercial motor vehicle unless he/she has first successfully completed a road test and has been issued a certificate of driver's road test in accordance with this regulation. It further requires that the road test be of sufficient duration to enable the person who administers it to evaluate the skill of the test taker at handling the commercial motor vehicle, and, at a minimum, the driver who takes the test must be tested while operating the type of commercial vehicle the motor carrier intends to assign to the driver, including the evaluation of pre-trip inspections required by § 392.7, which include coupling and uncoupling, use of controls and emergency equipment, passing, turning, braking, backing up, and completion of the road test form to rate the performance of the driver, which is also signed by the tested driver. Failure by the motor carrier to implement these duties and standards is an intentional and reckless failure to follow federally required safety systems. The failure to comply with the safety standards leads to death and injury of the motoring public.

A number of government and private studies of motor carriers and drivers has led to the conclusion that many motor carriers and their drivers fail to comply with hours-of-service regulations and cause the drivers to work longer than permitted. Working longer than permitted causes fatigue, which leads to accidents. The USDOT and the FMCSA conducted a safety study entitled the Comprehensive Safety Analysis (CSA), which was concluded in 2009 and then published in 2010. This study analyzed the FMCSA's Safety Challenge. The basic thesis of the study was that, "A growing carrier population and stable/unchanging FMCSA resources call for a more efficient and effective program." The study ultimately developed, "The Response CSA 2010." This included the development of a proactive safety program based on a scientific model that would do the following:

1) Promote accountability and strong enforcement as to priorities;
2) Extend FMCSA's reach to more carriers and drivers with safety problems;
3) Improve FMCSA's ability to identify safety problems earlier through better use of data.

This study was based in six states, including the state of Missouri, where 50 percent of the motor carrier population is covered. A system known as BASICS was developed. This acronym stands for the following:

Behavior **A**nalysis and **S**afety **I**mprovement **C**ategories
or **BASICs**
Unsafe Driving;
Fatigued Driving;
Driver Fitness;
Controlled Substances/Alcohol;
Vehicle Maintenance;
Improper Loading/Cargo;
Crash Indicator.

The CSA 2010 Comprehensive Intervention Process provides more tools to reach motor carriers and compel safety
compliance before crashes occur. This is done through a system of warning letters and investigations (including on-site
comprehensive investigations) to get enhanced compliance
review. It includes taking corrective actions requiring motor
carriers and drivers to be taken Out-of-Service (OOS) with
orders by the FMCSA. It further includes notices of violations to the motor carrier, notice of claims to the motor carrier, and provides for a Cooperative Safety Plan. In essence,
the FMCSA and this program attempt to predict crash indi-
cators through violation of safety systems and then study the
what, *why*, and *how* of the violation history of motor carriers
to determine why the system is breaking down. It then provides a procedural system for the motor carrier to address
their breakdowns and improve their safety record to prevent
further accidents from occurring.

One method of promoting safety and making drivers
comply with hours-of-service regulations is by the installation of electronic recorders onboard all commercial trucks
so that drivers comply with the FMCSR. The recorders erase
the need for handwritten logbooks, which can be easily fabricated. Many truck drivers carry two sets of books—one for
actual time and one to show law enforcement officers when
they are stopped for roadside safety checks.

Commercial Driver's License

Truck drivers in the past would employ the use of multiple driver's licenses from various states to avoid license suspension and other penalties. However, this changed with the enactment of the Commercial Motor Vehicle Safety Act of 1986. That law generally required that no person who operates a commercial motor vehicle shall at any time have more than one driver's license, except during the ten-day period beginning on the date such person is issued a driver's license and except where a state law enacted on or before June 1, 1986, requires such person to have more than one driver's license. This act greatly improved safety with motor carriers and truck drivers by implementing a safety-related rule that a commercial motor vehicle operator may not have more than one license, which allows government and state agencies to prevent bad truck drivers from operating on our nation's highways with multiple licenses. It has helped greatly in increasing uniformity among state licensing programs. With this act, the driving record of a driver can be checked promptly.

2

Number of
Trucks on US Roads

THE US TRUCKING industry is massive and comprises a large number of motor carriers. As of 2009, 26.4 million trucks were registered and used primarily for business purposes. This excludes the use of government and farm trucks and represents 24.4 percent of all the trucks registered. In 2009, the class 8 trucks used for business purposes was 2.4 million, as compared to 2.3 million class 8 trucks in 2010. The amount of commercial trailers registered in 2009 alone was 5.7 million. The companies involved in the trucking industry employ approximately 8.9 million people in trucking-related jobs, of which almost 3.5 million are truck drivers.

Accounting for almost 13.6 percent of America's truck sector are the LTL shippers. Out of the 3.5 million truck drivers employed, UPS employs almost sixty thousand workers. It is difficult to ascertain the exact number of trucks operating in the United States but it is estimated that as of today, 15.5 million trucks function on the roads, of which two million are tractor-trailers. Based on the statistics provided by the USDOT, as of 2010, the amount of people employed in the trucking industry was 6.8 million, and out of this figure, three million were truck drivers alone. Based on statistics provided by uShip.com in

2013, 761,850 tractor-trailer drivers were present, along with 49,920 light truck and delivery drivers, with an average salary of $37,770 annually.

Additionally, of the 3.5 million truck drivers present, one out of nine are sovereign and the majority of these are owner-operators. A large number of trucking companies function in the United States, both state-owned and private motor carriers. It is estimated that there are a total of 1.2 million trucking companies, out of which 97 percent function with twenty or fewer trucks and 90 percent work with six or fewer trucks. The number of trucks in the last ten years has increased greatly. In 1991, the approximate number of trucks in the United States was 4,480,815 and, as of 2011, this number has increased to 7,819,055 trucks. The trucking industry is massive and trucks are on the go twenty-four hours a day, seven days a week. Statistics on uShip.com for the year 2013 indicates that goods worth $139,463,000,000 were transported during that year by trucks. This means goods worth $382,090,411 per day and $4,422 per second were transported and shipped across our nation's highways.

Data collected from a number of sources helps us to determine the US truck fleet by use. As of 2012, the total number of trucks in fleet was 6,331,000, with 2,187,000 in business use, 1,560,000 in government use, and 465,000 in rental trucks (not including vans and SUVs). In order to provide a clearer idea as to the size of the trucks present on the US roads, the following data from 2002 categorizes trucks into three distinct categories—lightweight trucks, medium-weight trucks, and heavyweight trucks. All the weights are in pounds. As of 2002, the combined weight of all trucks present on the US roads was 85,174,000, with light trucks weighing 79,759,000 pounds, medium trucks weighing 1,914,000, and heavy trucks weighing 2,590,000.

The total estimated revenue generated by the US trucking industry is $255.5 billion, of which private fleets generated approximately $121 billion. The average operating ratio of trucking companies is 95.2, meaning that for each dollar in revenue, on average each trucking company incurs a cost of 95.2 cents, giving them a profit of 4.8 cents on every dollar. On average, a truck driver makes 30.3 cents per mile, for an average yearly income of $32,000. Out of the total fuel used by the transportation industry, trucks consume an average 53.9 billion gallons per year.

Number of Miles Driven by Trucks on US Roads

Trucking companies are carrying freight twenty-four hours a day, seven days a week. Research by the DOT found that Class 8 trucks travel billions of miles each year. Class 8 trucks are those that weigh thirty-three thousand pounds or more and are known as tractor-trailers. Statistics compiled from a number of sources show that in 2011, the number of miles traveled by trucks, particularly single-unit, two-axle, six-tire or more trucks was 103,515,000 miles.

Further research conducted on trucks specifically breaks down the total number of miles traveled in urban and rural areas. The total number of vehicle miles traveled in both rural and urban areas totaled 266,963,000 in 2007, of which 119,617,000 were rural highway and 107,346,000 were urban highway.

Furthermore, the total passenger miles in 2007 (in millions) was 226,963, out of which single-unit trucks traveled (in millions) 81,954 miles and combination trucks traveled 145,008 miles. Additionally, the average number of miles traveled by all trucks in 2007 (in millions) was 25,141. Single-unit trucks accounted for 12,040 miles, whereas combination trucks traveled 65,290 miles. The amount logged by all trucks in 2010, primarily for business purposes, was 397.8 billion miles. Of this amount, trucks alone traveled 29.8 percent. Class 6 and 8 trucks, in 2010, accounted for 131.2 billion miles, and in 2010 class 8 trucks alone traveled a total of 99.2 billion miles.

Trucks and motor carriers have a number of essential responsibilities and functions. One of the functions that has immense value to the overall economy is the delivery of raw material to manufacturers. Trucks are used for the transportation of raw materials from local suppliers (mines, farm, loggers, and quarries) to factories in order to turn the raw materials into vital products. After the manufacturing process is complete, the trucks are then required to transport the finished goods to retailers and wholesalers. Trucks carry all sorts of goods from one place to another and are responsible for $140 million in shipped goods annually, as of 2013, according to research conducted by Business Insider. The goods transported include furniture, motor vehicles, stone and minerals, agricultural and fish products, leathers, petroleum, textiles, wood, coal, and a number of other products. Trucks transport just about every product category that can be imagined.

Trucks deliver 70 percent of all the freight transported yearly in the United States. This accounts for $671 billion worth of manufactured and retail goods that are transported.

Average Speed
Along with miles traveled, it is also crucial to know the average speed at which drivers are allowed to operate on US interstate highways. This information is not only vital for truck drivers but also for all drivers on the road. A number of selected US interstate highways, along with their average truck-operating speeds, are below. The data is as of 2009:

Interstate Route	Average Speed in Miles per Hour
5	52.8
10	57.4
15	56.7

20	59.2
24	57.2
25	58.9
26	53.7
35	56.8
40	58.6
45	54.9

Hazardous Materials Transportation

Based on the data supplied by the USDOT, every year approximately four billion tons of dangerous materials are transported on the roads of the United States. This makes about five hundred thousand shipments on a daily basis. As of today, the government is working to ensure that strict standards for the transportation of dangerous materials are in place in order to achieve the utmost level of protection, not only for the trucks carrying the goods, but also for all vehicles sharing the roads with those trucks. A substantial portion of the hazardous materials carried by trucks is gasoline, fuel oil, diesel, liquid chemicals, and highly combustible elements and products. It is recommended that the federal government establish and mandate much more rigorous standards, especially for the transportation of nonradioactive dangerous materials.

Business Insider reports that almost eight hundred thousand truck drivers work in the United States and their combined earnings reach about $30 billion each year. The owner-operator model is mostly used by the small trucking businesses. This basically means that the truck driver is self-employed. Many larger motor carriers employ union drivers. The rights of each individual driver are protected by the unions. One of the largest unions is the Brotherhood of Teamsters. This union can have a substantial effect on the economy by simply striking. A prolonged strike in the trucking industry can bring the economy to a halt and can cause massive delays in shipping, along with sharp price increases. The effect of a shutdown is a higher end retail price for consumers.

It is further reported that the trucking industry accumulates revenues of $650 billion annually, meaning that it earns almost 84 percent of the entire revenue that is contributed by the commercial transportation industry. Due to the massive size of the US trucking industry, various regulations have been placed on it by federal, state, and local government. For example, regulations prevent trucks from driving on certain streets and roadways. Many state and federal agencies have set different speed limits for large trucks and tractor-trailers due to the hazards that go along with the transportation of goods. As discussed previously, maximum hours-of-service driving limits have been put in place to ensure the safety of the motoring public. Some motor carriers work together in coalitions to help shape the policies, regulations, and laws. They do this by creating minimum industry standards called *best practices* for the entire industry. One important organization that has considerable political power is the American Trucking Association. This association supplies relevant data and details about shipment, safety, and other information that helps the industry as a whole.

Despite the immense gross revenue of the US trucking industry, it still faces a number of challenges. The biggest concern faced by the industry is the fact that it is highly unsafe. Thousands of accidents are caused each year because of safety violations, combined with fatigued drivers and time deadlines imposed on tired truck drivers. The FMCSR and the CSA studies of the DOT and FMCSA are constantly undergoing changes to attempt to prevent fatal and life-altering injuries. Regardless of the rules and regulations that are presently in place, accidents still occur for a number of reasons.

3

SPECIFICATION OF TRUCKS ON US ROADS

THE LOGISTICS INDUSTRY, areas such as production, procurement, disposal, global, distribution, domestic, and concierge, is widespread and encompasses business logistics, which is composed of a number of segments of the business industry. The basic aim of logistics is to manage supply chains, the different stages of a project, and the subsequent efficiencies gained from it. It is crucial to have knowledge of the field of logistics for a number of reasons.

Logistics primarily deals with managing the flow of resources from the starting point to where the resource is consumed. Only by understanding the process of logistics can a company execute the delivery process perfectly and meet not only the requirements of the end customer but also the corporation. For many industries, logistics play a major role in enhancing the present production and distribution processes. By undertaking an efficient logistics operation, competitiveness and productivity can be increased. Transportation is a central aspect of logistics.

The reason why trucks are increasingly useful in commercial transportation is due to their ability to provide efficient circulation of all types of goods. The main aim behind truck-ing logistics is to guarantee that its operations are success-fully fulfilling the distinctive requirements of the trucking industry. People who work in the trucking logistics industry are responsible for not only examining the various trucking routes but also looking for ways to enhance efficiency and reduce delivery times.

In order to determine the best type of truck for the job, it is vital to classify the type and size of the load that needs to be transported. Due to the ever-increasing number of acci-dents caused by trucks, it becomes crucial to develop a good delivery plan, which includes determining the routes used, in order to ensure that drivers follow the FMCSR and rules on hours of service, as well as to ensure the safe transportation of the goods.

The logistics industry uses the popular tent vehi-cle plus trailer that carries a loading capacity of sixteen to twenty-five tons. This truck comes with a number of advantages, including the ability to provide fast loading and easy unloading, along with a greater loading volume. One drawback is its inability to be used for long-distance cargos. Another useful and popular truck used in this industry is the refrigerated truck, which is vital for the transportation of perishable goods. An isotherm truck is basically used for the transportation of food items. Various other trucks used in the logistics industry are the flatbed, trail life, semi-trailer, and the jumbo trailer truck.

Classes of Trucks

When a vehicle is manufactured, it is assigned a Gross Vehicle Weight Rating (GVWR). Based on this information, there are predominantly eight truck types on US roads as of today. The eight classes, along with the different types of trucks in each class, are as follows:

1. **Class 1: 6,000 and Less**
   - Minivan
   - Cargo van
   - SUV
   - Pickup Truck
2. **Class 2: 6,001 to 10,000**
   - Minivan
   - Cargo Van
   - Full-Size Pickup
   - Step Van
3. **Class 3: 10,001 to 14,000**
   - Walk-In
   - Box Truck
   - City Delivery
   - Heavy-Duty Pickup
4. **Class 4: 14,001 to 16,000**
   - Large Walk-In
   - Box Truck
   - City Delivery
5. **Class 5: 16,001 to 19,500**
   - Bucket Truck
   - Large Walk-In
   - City Delivery
6. **Class 6: 19,501 to 26,000**
   - Beverage Truck
   - Single-Axle
   - School Bus
   - Rack Truck
7. **Class 7: 26,001 to 33,000**
   - Refuse
   - Furniture
   - City Transit Bus
   - Truck Tractor

8. **Class 8: 33,001 & Over**
   - Cement Truck
   - Truck Tractor
   - Dump Truck
   - Sleeper

Types of Trucks

A number of different types of trucks function every day on US roads. The following trucks are categorized according to their capacity and the purpose they serve in transportation.

1. **Tent, semi-trailer:** This is the most common type of truck found on US roads and is used for a large variety of cargos. In these types of trucks, loading can take place either on the side of the truck or above it by removing the tent cover of the semi-trailer. This truck comprises a loading capacity of 20–25 tons with a useful volume of 60–92 cbm. They have a total capacity of 22–33 euro-pallets.

2. **Tent "jumbo":** This is another category of the semi-trailer but it has a larger capacity because of the "G" shape of the floor of the truck and the reduced diameter of the wheels. This truck comes with a loading capacity of 20 tons, a useful volume of 96–125 cbm, and a total capacity of 33 euro-pallets.

3. **Truck-trailer:** This type of truck is a combination of a truck trailer and a tent. The main advantage of this truck type is the fast loading and unloading that it offers, along with a large, useful loading volume. However, its weak point is the fact that it is unsuitable for the tranportation of long-distance cargos.

The total loading capacity of this truck is 16–25 tons, with a total capactiy of 22–33 euro-pallets and a useful volume of 60–12 cbm.

4. **Refrigerated truck/frigo:** This is a semi-trailer and is used for the transportation of perishable goods. It comes with special storage conditions that allow a temperature range of +250C to -250C. The loading capacity of this truck is 12–22 tons, with a useful volume of 60–92 cbm. It carries a total capacity of 24–33 euro-pallets. The European standard it carries is up to 20 tons of 82 cbm and 32 euro-pallets.

5. **Isotherm:** This is a form of a semi-trailer and can also be classified as a truck-trailer and separate truck. The intended use of this type of truck is for the transportation of food, as it is able to keep a certain temperature for a long amount of time. This truck comes with a loading capacity of 3–25 tons and a useful volume of 32–92 cbm. It has a capacity of 6–33 euro-pallets.

6. **Flatbed Truck:** This truck type is used for the transportation of goods that stand steady against external influences. An advantage of this type of truck is that it can be used for the transportation of oversized cargos. The total loading capacity of this truck is 15–25 tons.

7. **Flatbed and Low-Bed Trucks:** This truck type is useful in the transportation of oversized cargos and has a total loading capacity of 20–40 tons.

8. **Lorry Tank:** This truck is used for the transportation of food and nonfood liquid products. It comes with a loading capacity of 12–20 tons and a useful volume of 6–40 cbm.

9. **Timber Lorry:** This truck type is useful for the transportation of forest products and comes with a loading capacity of 10–20 tons.

Truck Consumption

Of the eight truck classes identified above, the heaviest trucks consume an average of 6.5 gallons per thousand ton miles. Below is a comparison of the different truck classes, their weights, and fuel consumption. Cars and small pickups, vans, and sport-utility vehicles (SUVs) are shown here for comparison. Two truck classes are further subdivided into categories "a" and "b." Based on the GVWR, class 2 trucks are subdivided into classes 2a and 2b, and class 8 trucks are subdivided into classes 8a and 8b, based on the design of the truck (straight truck vs. combination truck)

Class	Applications	Gross Weight Range (lbs.)	Typical fuel consumed (gallons per thousand tonmiles)
1c	Cars only	3200-6000	69.0
1t	Minivans, small SUVs, small pickups	4000-6000	58.8
2a	Large SUVs, standard pickups	6001-8500	38.5
2b	Large pickups, utility van, multi-purpose, minibus, step van	8,501-10,000	38.5

3	Utility van, multipur- pose, minibus, step van	10,001-14,000	33.3
4	City delivery, parcel delivery, large walk-in, landscaping, bucket	14,001-16,000	23.8
5	City delivery, parcel delivery, large walk-in, landscaping, bucket	16,001-19,500	25.6
6	City delivery, school bus, large walk-in, bucket	19,501-26,000	20.4
7	City bus, furniture, refrigerated, dump, fuel tanker, tow, fire engine, tractor-trailer	26,001-33,000	18.2
8a	Straight trucks, e.g. dump, refuse, concrete, furniture, city, bus, tow, fire engine	33,001-80,000	8.7
8b	Combination truck, e.g. tractor-trailer: van, refrig- erated, bulk tanker, flatbed	33,001-80,000	6.5

Location of Truck Assembly Plants

Medium and heavy truck assembly plants are located throughout the United States. Predominantly, there are seven major manufacturers of class 7 and class 8 trucks in the United States. They are Freightliner, Star, Hino, International, Kenworth, Mack, Peterbilt, and Volvo. Of these manufacturers, Freightliner and International also manufacture medium trucks (classes 3–6), along with Isuzu. Below is a table showing the production of medium and heavy trucks by manufacturer name (data is as of 2012):

Freightliner and Western Start	Hino	Interna- tional	Kenworth	Mack	Peterbilt	Volvo	Isuzu
56.9	8.2	41.0	32.7	25.0	29.4	26.1	2.6

Sales

- As of 2012, class 3 truck sales were up. Class 3 truck sales fell, along with the economy, in 2008 and 2009 but soon recovered in 2010 and through 2012. Sales in 2012 were higher by approximately 19 percent than sales in 2008. The market dominators in the class 3 truck category were Chrysler, Ford, and General Motors.
- As of 2012, class 4–7 truck sales were below those of 2008. Despite the fact that they continued to grow in 2012, they were still 5 percent below the sales level of 2008. As for General Motors, in 2008 they sold twenty-five thousand class 4–7 trucks, whereas in 2012 they sold none.
- In 2012, class 8 truck sales continued to grow, doubling the amount sold in 2009. As of 2012, Freightliner had 34 percent of the market and International had 18 percent. All other companies had less than a 15 percent share of the market.

Combination Trucks

Based on research conducted by the Federal Highway Administration (FHA), the average miles traveled per truck for a combination truck in 2011 was approximately sixty-six thousand. The average miles traveled by these trucks have large standard deviations every year because the duty cycles of these trucks greatly vary.

4

TRUCK ACCIDENT STATISTICS

B ETWEEN 1995 AND 1998, the death toll due to large-truck accidents increased by 10 percent. The figure rose from 4,918 deaths in 1995 to approximately 5,374 deaths in 1998. Large trucks include a number of categories, such as tractor-trailers, certain heavy cargo vans, and single-unit trucks that weigh more than ten thousand pounds. These vehicles account for an inexplicably large number of traffic deaths based on the number of miles traveled. For large trucks, a deadly crash rate exists at a statistical level of 2.6 deaths per one hundred million vehicle miles traveled. This statistic is 50 percent more than the rate of all other road vehicle accidents combined.

Special consideration has been given by the FMCSA regarding the research on accidents between large trucks (weighing over 4,540 kilograms) and other vehicles on the road. The main purpose of this research is to increase awareness of the risky behaviors by both truck drivers and passenger vehicle drivers. Going back over a decade, as of 1998, large trucks were responsible for 7 percent of the entire vehicle miles covered and were a cause of approximately 13 percent of all traffic fatalities. In such accidents, 78 percent of the deaths were of the injured car drivers and/or passengers. Based on research conducted in 1998, and after examining the Fatality Analysis Reporting System (FARS), it was concluded that a car driver's driving behavior was three times more likely to cause fatal crashes as compared to that of truck drivers.

One reason that greatly contributes to crashes is the fact that the general public sharing the roads with heavily loaded tractors and trailers is unaware that these trucks cannot stop in the same distance as passenger cars. The Insurance Institute for Highway Safety (IIHS) reported that large trucks, which included single-unit and tractor-trailers with weight in excess of ten thousand pounds, cause far more deaths on the highway than passenger cars in general. The institute reports that these heavy commercial motor vehicles have a higher incident rate per mile when it comes to deaths than passenger vehicles. Passenger vehicle occupants obviously are at greater risk for death simply due to how force and mass, combined with speed and acceleration, affect smaller and weaker vehicles. The larger the mass of the truck and trailer, the more deadly the force is at the moment of impact. On average, trucks weigh twenty to thirty times more than passenger cars. The motoring public in a car will always be the loser when a collision occurs, and the smaller vehicle takes the brunt of the impact. Truck drivers in larger vehicles often walk away from an accident unscathed, while the occupants of the cars leave in body bags.

Accident Statistics

Trucking revenues are growing fast. While this is good news for trucking companies and the economy as a whole, it is disadvantageous for all other vehicles that travel with these trucks, as it raises the potential threat of truck-related accidents and deaths.

A number of agencies in the United States are responsible for reporting and tracking truck-driving statistics. These agencies fall under the USDOT and include National Highway Traffic Safety Administration (NHTSA), Federal Highway Administration (FHA), and the FMCSA.

Regulation of the interstate commercial driving safety requirements and of the interstate commercial driver license requirements are all undertaken by the FMCSA. The job of the FHA is to ensure that all trucks obey rules and regulations, such as the limitation on the size and weight of the vehicle. This has to be monitored closely in order to protect the infrastructure of the highways and to improve the safety of trucks. Reporting of tractor-trailer accidents and roadside violations of the FMCSR is primarily performed by the NHTSA and the FMCSA, while the basic job of the FHA is to provide information regarding trucking statistics, such as freight tonnage carried across the nation's highways. The Insurance Institute for Highway Safety (IIHS) undertakes the tracking of truck accidents, including fatalities and injury numbers, for the Highway Safety Coalition and the Truck Safety Coalition.

As a parent agency, the DOT reported the following statistics related to trucking accidents in the United States:

- As of December 2010, more than 1.1 million interstate motor carriers were present. The motor carriers include for-hire, private carriers, business fleets, and owner-operators.
- According to the last available data of 2007, the Commodity Flow Survey reported that trucks carried and transported goods that were worth more than $8.3 trillion.
- The approximate tonnage of freight moved each year is eleven billion.
- The number of large truck occupiers that died in 2009 was 529.
- The number of truck occupiers injured in 2009 was twenty thousand.
- On an annual basis, five hundred thousand truck-related accidents occur.

- In 2010, 1.1 serious crashes took place per one hundred million truck miles.

The statistics tend to vary depending on the reporting authority, but it is a widely accepted fact that truck crashes are increasingly common and the number of fatalities is rising as well. The IIHS reported the following statistics as of 2010:

- The total number of truck miles traveled was 286,585 million.
- The number of deaths due to large trucks totaled 3,413 people.
- Of this number of deaths, 14 percent were truck occupants and 72 percent were occupants in passenger cars.
- Pedestrians, bicyclists, and motorcyclists accounted for 13 percent of the deaths.
- As compared to 2009, the number of deaths in 2010 rose by a staggering 8 percent.
- The share of large trucks in these accidents was almost 4 percent of the registered vehicles and 9 percent of the total deaths due to motor vehicle crashes.
- Deaths caused by tractor-trailers was 75 percent while 25 percent were caused by single large trucks.

Of all the car accidents in 2012, commercial trucks were involved in 2.4 percent of them. It has been estimated that the rate of truck driver-caused crashes is very high, with one person killed or injured every sixteen minutes. Based on research by the USDOT, it is estimated that five hundred thousand accidents involving trucks occur each year. The major cause of 75 percent of these truck accidents is the fault of the drivers of passenger vehicles and only 16 percent of all truck accidents are the fault of the truck driver. The number of people killed every year in truck accidents is almost five thousand.

Approximately 98 percent of the time, the person killed is in the other vehicle, not in the larger truck or tractor-trailer.

Approximately 68 percent of truck accidents occur in rural areas as opposed to urban areas. Of this percentage, 68 percent happen during the daytime and 78 percent occur on the weekends. The states that account for the highest number of truck accidents are California, Florida, Texas, Pennsylvania, and Georgia.

Statistics indicate that some 1,159 accidents occurred in Oregon, which resulted not only in severe injuries and in damages to vehicles, but also caused many deaths. This number is 8.01 percent higher than it was in 2003. Of this number, 621 truck accidents were due to the fault of the truck driver. The maximum number of truck accidents increased to thirteen accidents per day and the largest number of accidents caused by one trucking company was twenty-six accidents. Of the 1,159 accidents, 3.02 percent of the trucks were carrying hazardous materials when the accidents took place.

As mentioned earlier, trucks weigh almost thirty times more than passenger vehicles. This points toward only one harsh reality: In truck and tractor-trailer related accidents, the people most likely to die are those in the passenger vehicles. The stopping distance required by trucks is far greater than that required by cars, especially when the trucks are heavily loaded. We can conclude that drivers of passenger cars need to be aware of two crucial issues. First, heavily loaded trucks and tractor-trailers are dangerous. Second, an overloaded truck or tractor-trailer will require a much greater stopping distance than a properly loaded truck or tractor-trailer.

A 2006 study called, "The Large-Truck Crash Causation Study: An Initial Overview," published by the NHTSA, analyzed the major causes of truck-related accidents, and some common variables or factors contributing to crashes, injuries, and deaths. The study analyzed 2,284 vehicles involved in

1,070 crashes, and over one thousand variables. Some of the variables included vehicle type, weight, cargo type, brakes, air bag status, driving records of drivers, fatigue factors, sleep patterns (also known as circadian rhythms), and seat belt and other restraint systems. One of the key terms was a, "critical event," defined as the event that immediately led to the crash. The critical event is the action or event that made the crash unavoidable, and only one critical event was defined for each crash.

This study evaluated the following accident types:

A. Right roadside departure;
B. Rear-end collision;
C. Turn-across path;
D. Straight paths;
E. Same Trafficway Same Direction, Forward Impact;
F. Same Trafficway Opposite Directions, Forward Impact;
G. Turn-into Path;
H. Single Driver, Forward Impact;
I. Same Trafficway Same Direction, Sideswipe/Angle;
J. Miscellaneous types of accidents.

This study found many causation-related issues with truck crashes, some of which are discussed below.

- A tire bursting is one of the most common critical reasons why crashes occur with large trucks. This obviously leads to the conclusion that the motor carrier industry needs to have better systems of maintenance and repair as required under the FMCSR pre-trip daily inspections. Tires are often not replaced on a timely basis due to the associated cost of replacement, which ultimately reduces the motor carrier's or truck driver's profitability. In other words, driving on worn tires saves money, makes more profit per mile, but has high costs associated with crashes, injuries, and deaths to car occupants.

- Engine problems can be included in the category of disabling or non-disabling vehicle failure. This again relates to poor maintenance and repair in order to increase profits at the cost of human lives.

- Deteriorating or inadequate road conditions that may be due to poor weather conditions or a lack of maintenance by state, federal, and county highway departments can cause accidents if vehicles are not traveling at safe and appropriate speeds for the specific road conditions.

- Sudden shifts of truck cargo can cause a truck to lose control. These accidents can be prevented by following the FMCSR rules on cargo loading and the CSA study about cargo loading and weight, since it is known that poorly loaded cargo will shift and cause accidents.

- Lane drifting is a critical event that causes many accidents. The motorist in a passenger car should always be observant of large trucks and tractor-trailers lane shifting. Trucks can shift because of weather conditions like heavy winds, which can cause them to lose control and leave the traveled roadway.

- Truck drivers that are not properly qualified and trained on defensive driving techniques, hazard perception, and awareness techniques may have difficulty when making turns at intersections or when simply passing through intersections, and may cause accidents.

- Heavily loaded trucks may not be able to stop for traffic that slows or stops ahead of the truck's path. When the truck driver is operating too fast for slowed or stopped traffic, a critical event occurs and a crash becomes a reality.

- Intoxicated drivers are a major cause of crashes and deaths.
- Driver fatigue is a problem that results in injury and deaths to other motorists.
- Objects left on the highway from improperly loaded truck cargo cause critical events that lead to crashes.

According to a 1994 report by the NHTA, truck driver fatigue is a contributing factor in approximately 30 percent to 40 percent of all large truck accidents. A study in 1995 by the National Transportation Safety Board (NTSB) found that in 107 heavy truck crashes, fatigue was a critical factor 75 percent of the time. For those drivers who do not comply with the FMCSR and associated state regulations and stay on the roads for more than the number of hours permitted, they are twice as likely to crash and cause accidents than those drivers who drive for the regulated amount of time.

The large number of statistics regarding truck-related accidents indicates an overwhelming need for additional safety and hours-of-service regulations. The bottom line is that trucks are, without a doubt, the cause of thousands of accidents each year. The numerous federal and state agencies are doing their best in the promotion of truck safety, but there has to be an increase in public awareness about the dangers of truck drivers and motor carriers that operate with a careless system aimed at on-time delivery rather than road safety.

Tips for Sharing the Road with Trucks
1. **Truck-wise:** It is essential for vehicles sharing the road with trucks to be able to identify the different types of trucks in order to maximize safety.

- Oversize trucks: These trucks are not like the average trucks you see. They are longer, wider, and larger than average trucks. These trucks use flashing orange lights and the lights are usually present in the front and the back in order to allow vehicles to see the size and potential hazard of these oversized monster trucks.
- Long vehicles: These vehicles have the ability to tow a number of different types of trailers that can actually be the length of two semis. These longer tractor-trailers are especially dangerous due to the increased stopping distance of the tandem trailers. These tractor-trailers make wider turns than normal tractor-trailers. They carry more cargo. Because of increased weight and mass, they are especially hazardous to cars.

2. **Do not cut in:** It is critical that drivers in cars avoid large trucks and the blind spots associated with them. Keep an appropriate distance in front of and behind these dangerous trucks.

3. **Do not overtake a turning vehicle:** All types of trucks require a wider space for turning, especially larger trucks, and in many areas, trucks can legally turn from the center lane. Never move into the blind spot of a truck, especially when it is turning. Always remember that if you cannot see the driver's face in the mirrors, he or she cannot see you either.

4. **Maintain your speed:** Drivers should be extremely cautious when driving next to trucks, especially when a truck is overtaking. Avoid staying immediately next to a large truck or tractor-trailer in the adjacent lane. As previously noted, wind and other weather conditions can cause them to have sudden lane shifts. Poorly trained or underqualified drivers are not good

at maintaining a single lane of travel. It's best to allow them to pass quickly and then keep a safe and appropriate distance.

5. **Roundabouts**: Operators of passenger cars need to take note of the recent increase in the construction of roundabouts. The larger trucks will shift lanes while going through these types of intersections. Again, keep a safe distance. Large trucks need wider spaces to make turns and require a larger turning radius or area. You should stay far away from trucks in these types of roadways in order to protect yourself, your family, and other passengers.

5

Maintenance Problems and Lack of Driver Training in the Trucking Industry

THE INADEQUATE MAINTENANCE **of trucks is a direct cause of truck accidents. A substantial number of truck crashes are a direct result of mechanical failures in the tractors and/or trailers. These mechanical failures are due to the motor carrier's failure to conduct appropriate daily inspections of the equipment and repair failing, broken, and defective equipment.**

Braking defects are the most common deficiency that leads to truck accidents. The brakes of a truck may cease to function or may not work with the required strength because they become oil-contaminated. Drivers often overlook defects in brakes because they conduct inadequate daily pre-trip inspections. When a driver does a pre-trip inspection, he must log all findings. It is at the driver's discretion to overlook a defect if he finds one and commence driving a big rig in an unsafe condition.

Tire inspections should be performed on a daily basis. Not performing these inspections will ultimately lead to a blowout. Motorists on the nation's highways often see portions of blown-out tires from tractor-trailers. That is often caused by inadequate inspections and a lack of maintenance. The truck drivers often will notice that tread depth is at a very dangerous level. Rather than spend the required money that it would take to replace the tire, they fail to write down the finding on the log and start their trip. A blowout occurs and then the obvious happens. The tractor unit loses control or another motorist has an accident by coming upon the remnants of the stripped tire in the roadway. Safety concerns demand that the drivers perform the appropriate pre-trip inspection on a regular basis.

Wheel separations due to improperly fitted wheel and hub assemblies can cause truck accidents. Because wheel separations are a known and foreseeable occurrence, motor carriers are required to inspect for problems. When the period of inspection lags, the repair and maintenance is put off and accidents occur. Maintenance of the tractor and trailer is the duty of the motor carrier and the driver. The driver has a separate duty to inspect the tractor-trailer before leaving for a new destination and at specified intervals per the FMCSR. All of these factors fall under issues of proper repair and maintenance.

Part 392.7 of the FMCSR on equipment inspection requires that no commercial motor vehicle shall be driven unless the driver is satisfied that the following parts and accessories are in good working order, nor shall the driver fail to use or make use of such parts and accessories as needed:

1. Service brakes, including trailer brake connections
2. Parking (hand) brake
3. Steering mechanism
4. Lighting devices and reflectors
5. Tires
6. Horn
7. Windshield wipers

8. Rear-vision mirrors
9. Coupling devices

Subparagraph (b) of this regulation requires that the drivers operating the equipment over the road shall be deemed to have confirmed that the components were in good working order at the time that they accepted the equipment and made a decision to commence driving. In addition to all of the parts listed above, they must also check wheels, airline connections, kingpin upper coupling devices, rails or supporting frames, tie-down bolsters, locking pins, clamps, and sliding frame locks, as well as many other parts.

The FMCSR requires the driver and carrier to keep maintenance and repair logs so that in the event of an accident, the FMCSA, highway patrol and other police officers can properly perform an inspection to help determine why the accident occurred in the first place. When drivers are stopped for roadside inspections by law officers, and bad violations are found, they will issue specific citations for violating regulations of the FMCSR. When the violations are severe, the driver and truck will be taken out of service. These violations are sent to the FMCSA, where the specific carrier information is maintained on all trucks that a motor carrier has driving for it. This allows a safety rating to be assigned to the motor carrier for their maintenance history.

Any person or company can go to the following link and view the motor carrier's maintenance history by inserting the carrier name or the motor carrier's DOT number.

https://safer.fmcsa.dot.gov/CompanySnapshot.aspx
This allows the federal government, state government, police officers, and safety professionals, as well as lawyers bringing claims for injured victims of trucking accidents to perform an immediate search of the carrier's past maintenance history. All of the citations are identified on the search pages. An individual

searching here can review and print all applicable similar maintenance infractions. This allows the reviewing person or government entity to determine if the motor carrier has developed a habit and custom of failing to repair equipment. If a motor carrier's rating of violations becomes high enough, the carrier will be red flagged for a review and a government audit occurs.

The motor carrier has a duty, as does the driver, to keep the maintenance process logged and recorded properly. They are required to perform safety repairs when necessary and required. As noted above, as the rate of violations rises due to roadside inspections and accidents, the motor carrier's rating becomes higher and higher. The end result of the government's Safer System website is to try to have a prophylactic preventative system to identify motor carriers who do not follow the FMCSR. When an audit occurs, if the motor carrier fails to comply with the request from the DOT and the FMCSR, then the motor carrier may lose its operating authority under the DOT. When a motor carrier loses its operating authority, they are unable to transport goods throughout the United States on any highway, street, or roadway.

A motor carrier can maintain its appropriate authority and license to operate by simply taking a tractor-trailer out of service for a period of time to make the appropriate repairs. The reason that this is not done, on the occasions where a motor carrier fails to comply with the rules, is because a loss of profit occurs when the tractor-trailer is unable to move goods across the highways. A conscious decision has to be made by the driver and/or the motor carrier to put off maintenance and repairs until another day. This reckless decision is a primary cause of injury and death in truck accidents. The truck driver is in the best possible position when he inspects the truck on a daily basis.

The decision not to pay for the necessary repairs is one that is primarily made by the driver. However, the driver may be at the beck and call of the motor carrier. Sometimes, good drivers call their dispatch officers and inform them about the need for a repair and are told to continue driving the load so that the load is delivered on time. Drivers become fearful of losing their jobs due to reprimands, terminations, reduced pay, and lost bonuses. The system developed by the motor carrier that punishes the driver ultimately causes injury and death to other motorists. The duty of the driver and the motor carrier is combined. The trucking company and the driver are typically called the "motor carrier." Both must obey the same regulations in order to prevent injury and operate safely.

Trucking organizations are obliged to follow the safety rules promulgated by the DOT and the FMCSA. The FMCSA set forth the required rules and regulations under Chapter 49 of the Code of Federal Regulations. The applicable sections are from section 380 to section 399. FMCSA regulation, part 396, requires that trucking and transport organizations examine their trucks, tractors, and trailers for maintenance. A qualified maintenance supervisor is obligated to analyze and examine all trucks in the organization's fleet at regular intervals and at a minimum of one time per year. The maintenance and repair investigation is a requirement that makes it mandatory that the motor carrier perform a thorough and complete inspection. The inspection requirement under part 396.3 requires that every motor carrier, and Intermodal equipment provider systematically inspect, repair, and maintain, or cause to be systematically inspected, repaired, and maintained, all motor vehicles and Intermodal equipment that are subject to the motor carrier's control. This part requires that all parts and accessories be in safe and proper operating condition at all times.

Part 396.7 forbids unsafe operation. It generally requires that a motor vehicle shall not be operated in such condition as to be likely to cause an accident or a breakdown of the vehicle.

The FMCSA regulations, parts 393 and 396, require that all commercial trucks be legitimately maintained and repaired. The rules refer to specific maintenance issues that are known to be likely to cause accidents. Some of them are:

- Inoperative Vehicle Lights: These incorporate turn signals, taillights, and headlamps.
- Defective Lights: Retro-reflective stripping.
- Tire Tread: The truck tire tread should not be less than 2/32 of an inch.
- Trailer Lights: All trailer lights must be in working operation and visible.
- Oil or Grease Leaks: The truck should not be spilling oil or grease.

The appropriate maintenance of trucks, both large trucks and semi-trucks, can mean the difference between life and death to smaller passenger vehicles on the roads. When the driver and motor carrier fail to properly maintain the vehicles, it will lead to accidents, causing human misery, suffering, and death. One reported accident that occurred in Caddo County, Oklahoma, a few years ago provides an example of what can happen due to improper maintenance. In this particular accident, a semi had its rear axle come loose, which led to losing the tires and the capability of staying in the appropriate lane of travel. The driver obviously lost control. The duals of the fifth axle flew into the windshield of a passing vehicle and two teenagers were killed. The location of the accident was in a rural area. Emergency responders were not able to get to the site crash until a lengthy period of time later. By then, it was too late to save the occupants of the vehicle. This type of accident is preventable. Simple, appropriate maintenance, inspection, and repair would have prevented the axle from breaking. It is quite likely that the driver knew or reasonably should have known that the vehicle was not operating properly. Rather than shut down the vehicle and inspect the tractor-trailer, the driver chose to continue operation. Again, the driver and carrier have on-time requirements that make them ignore the obvious need for repairs.

As the costs of maintenance and repair increase, the frequency of maintenance and repair decrease, which leads to injuries on highways. The importance of the motor carrier developing a safety inspection and maintenance program to comply with the FMCSR cannot be ignored. One of the best ways to prevent accidents is to make certain that the driver performs daily pre-trip inspections. The motor carrier must perform their interval inspections as required. Annual inspections must be performed by qualified personnel who are trained to inspect and repair each and every part that may be defective. Accidents that are caused by mechanical failures are almost always preventable. Inspection and maintenance should lead to discovery of the defect or need for repair. For the motor carrier, taking the time and money necessary to stop the truck for a day, week, or month and bring it out of service would obviously lead to a loss of gross revenue. However, following the requirements would lead to a safe tractor-trailer operating on the roadways. In turn, the chance of a motor vehicle accident would be lessened.

There are a number of measures that can be taken by trucking companies, especially those dealing with semi-trucks, to ensure that their vehicles are properly maintained:

- A proper record-keeping system should be in place for timely maintenance, which records details of inspections and repairs performed on the trucks.
- Motor carriers and drivers must be trained and supervised to know exactly when a truck is required to be taken out of service instead of waiting for roadside police inspections and/or accidents.

- Motor carriers should purchase texts or manuals known as the Management Edition of the FMCSR, similar to the manual produced by TransProducts. com, which provides interpretive guidelines to follow the FMCSR. The appropriate safety and maintenance personnel then must be trained through appropriate classroom and video training to understand and comprehend the regulations so that an effective plan can be implemented. Drivers need to be trained on the very same information so that the driver understands when a motor vehicle must be taken out of service.
- Motor carriers must develop a system of providing training to drivers to ensure they understand the current applicable regulations. The drivers then need to be tested on a weekly or monthly basis to determine their comprehension of the rules. Carriers know that many drivers do not read the information they provide. Only testing will determine if the driver has appropriately paid attention to the training that is supposedly being given. When a motor carrier fails to test the drivers on new information, they are turning a blind eye to safety.
- Maintenance personnel must be taught to look for defects in the truck's suspension, couplers, brakes, tires, wheels, and steering.
- Companywide meetings, known as safety meetings, should be held on a weekly basis, followed by written comprehensive testing. This will help to eliminate the drivers who either will not read or learn the rules or are too incompetent to follow them.

Driver inspections are required under part 396.13 of the regulations. They require the driver to be satisfied that the motor vehicle is in safe operating condition before driving it. The driver is required to review the last driver vehicle inspection report. The driver is required to sign the report if defects or deficiencies are noted by the last driver. The driver is also required to sign the report to certify that required repairs have been performed.

Periodic inspections are required under part 396.17. The inspection must include, at a minimum, parts and accessories set forth in appendix G of that subchapter. This part requires that a motor carrier must not use a commercial motor vehicle and an Intermodal equipment provider must not tender equipment to a motor carrier for interchange, unless each component identified in appendix G of that subchapter has passed an inspection in accordance with the terms of the section at least one time during the preceding twelve-month period. It requires documentation of the inspection on the vehicle and must comply with part 396.21(a). It must also include the date of the inspection, the name of the motor carrier, and information uniquely identifying the vehicle inspected. It must certify that the vehicle passed an inspection in accordance with section 396.17. A penalty is set forth under (h), which states that the failure to perform the annual inspection properly shall cause a motor carrier or the Intermodal equipment provider to be subject to the penalty provisions of 49 U.S.C. 521(b).

Periodic main inspections (PMI) are required to be performed as noted in the preceding section. The annual periodic maintenance inspection requirement is a minimum requirement under the FMCSR. Motor carriers should not simply follow a minimum guideline. In order to operate safely, it is suggested that motor carriers set up a quarterly inspection interval at the very least. This would provide prophylactic procedures to look for parts that are about to become defective or expire. Tires can be replaced early. Axles and other similar connective devices can be checked more frequently to prevent their failure.

The combination of daily vehicle inspections and periodic maintenance inspections is a safety system designed by the federal government and safety experts to assist in preventing accidents. The more often the inspections are done, the safer the tractor-trailer will be on the roads. When a vehicle has a high level of breakdowns, it becomes apparent that the vehicle should be taken out of service or perhaps discontinued as an in-service vehicle. Vehicles reach a point where repairs become too costly. At that time, the motor carrier should make the appropriate financial expenditures to purchase new equipment and completely discontinue and abandon use of the old equipment. IRS guidelines for depreciation allow for different schedules of depreciation. One of the points of bonus depreciation is to help companies improve the quality of their equipment while enjoying the benefits of accelerated depreciation.

One of the reasons why maintenance regulations and inspections may not be followed deals with driver compensation. Drivers often ignore the need for maintenance and repair because they lose money while their truck is being repaired. Sometimes motor carriers will reprimand or terminate drivers if they report the need for safety repairs. Motor carriers should set up a different type of system of pay that is not based on a "per mile" or "on-time" delivery system. A driver should be paid their normal weekly rate while a vehicle is taken out of service and repaired. This would allow the driver to provide for his family and eliminate thousands, if not millions, of unnecessary and preventable tractor-trailer accidents. Profit-driven protocols of motor carriers create unsafe operating conditions. Failing to pay a driver while the driver is out of service creates a situation where the driver is forced to drive an unsafe vehicle simply to avoid losing pay. This unsafe system must change in order to have any improvement in the safe operation of tractor-trailers and large trucks.

The compensation rate of the mechanics and maintenance inspectors is another reason why unsafe trucks continue to operate on the road. Motor carriers are capable of paying a higher level of compensation to their qualified maintenance inspectors. Their decision to pay the mechanic a lower rate like $15 an hour leads to the result that the employee may not perform the same level of work as a mechanic who is paid $35 an hour. The motor carrier is in charge of the timeframe that the mechanic is allowed to spend for each category of inspection and repair. In the event that the motor carrier decides to allow a longer period of time to the mechanic for each category of inspection, it will increase the cost of the inspection. Developing a system that sets an average period of time that is sufficient to perform a realistic inspection for each category of parts and equipment that must be inspected and that pays a fair labor rate to the mechanic or inspector will lead to a much more thorough inspection. Accidents will be prevented if appropriate inspections are conducted. In other words, rapid, cheap inspections lead to accidents. Careful and appropriate inspections lead to safety and less injuries and deaths.

Motor Carrier Safety Assistance Program

The Motor Carrier Safety Assistance Program (MCSAP), introduced in 1982, has been a great help, especially with inspection of trucks to determine whether they comply with the FMCSR. After the inception of this program, vehicle compliance has increased by a factor of ten. Despite this, the number of drivers and motor carriers that are receiving out-of-service citations for violating the FMCSR has not lessened. The program also has a major drawback. Because the FMCSA has limited funds and personnel, they are only able to inspect a small number of trucks on the roads. In order for the MCSAP to gain full advantage, the program has to be solidified both at the state and federal levels. Only then can a larger number of vehicles and drivers be inspected.

When trucks are overloaded or improperly loaded with cargo, they become a great danger to all drivers using the nation's highways. It would be highly beneficial to include size and weight restrictions in the MCSAP inspections in order to decrease the danger to persons using the federal and state highway systems.

Truck Conspicuity and Lighting Display

The regulations regarding truck lighting requirements have not been updated in a long time. These requirements come from the FMCSR. Many accidents occur in poor-visibility or dark conditions because motorists are unable to properly see large trucks and tractor-trailers. Many trucks have inadequate exterior lighting. Drivers who experience lower contrast sensitivity and inferior night vision are not able to identify trucks with low-level conspicuity and lighting. The FMCSR conspicuity requirements can be found at 49 CFR 393.9 *et. seq.* and provide regulations for lamps, reflective devices, and electrical wiring.

Section 393.11 has a table that provides guidance to truck drivers and motor carriers on how to properly use lighting, lamps, and conspicuity tape. The problem with the rules is that truck drivers are not always properly trained on them and the motor carrier does not always understand them. These federal regulations should be strengthened to require motor carriers to spend the necessary monies to provide appropriate warnings to motorists in nighttime and poor-visibility conditions. This will lessen the amount of crashes and, in turn, reduce deaths and injuries to motorists in cars.

Truck Tires

Truck tires are a leading cause of accidents. Truck drivers and motor carriers must set up vehicle and tire inspection and repair safety programs and actually implement and follow them in order to have any useful prevention of accidents from worn tires. Rules need to be followed to make certain that tires are replaced, and that rebuilt and retreaded tires are not used by large trucks. Trucks need to have the best quality tires. It is recommended that regulations be set in place that determine the highest quality truck tires are embedded with the right details, such as carcass design and tread depth. If these rules are created, implemented, and followed, accidents will be prevented. Stopping distances of large trucks will be improved. The motor carrier will benefit by increased fuel efficiency and profits.

Blown out Tires

Blown out tires left on a roadway are known as hazards. They create a significant hazard and danger to all persons using the nation's highways, regardless of whether they are in a passenger car, a motorcycle, or other type of vehicle. They are more dangerous at nighttime due to lower visibility. Many truck drivers will have tires blow out and continue to drive the tractor-trailer down the roadway without picking up the remnants of the tires. Some of these tires are so large that the remnants create objects that are hazards in the roadway. At nighttime, motorists may not see the object until the last minute and then veer to avoid the object, which leads to collisions and accidents. At other times, the motorist will run over the large remnants of tires, which may cause their vehicle to veer and leave the roadway. It is thought that tire blowouts on roadways cause in excess of twenty-five thousand accidents per year and at least one hundred deaths every year in the United States and Canada. The AAA Foundation for Traffic Safety has reported that tire blowout hazards are an overwhelming danger to motorists and create problematic situations that are unavoidable.

Tire Blowout of Mechanical Origin

A tire blowout from a mechanical origin involves a defect with the tire or rim and the quality of the assembly of the tire onto the rim. These types of blowouts are especially dangerous and hazardous. An enormous energy burst arises from the blowout, which causes the tractor-trailer to lose control. The driver of the tractor-trailer may not anticipate the shifting of the tractor-trailer and all cargo. The tractor-trailer can easily veer into oncoming lanes of travel, shift into adjacent lanes of travel, and, at times, can cause the truck driver to drive off the traveled roadway where the truck driver is injured and/or killed.

There are four events of mechanical origin that can cause a tire to blow out. They are:

a. Over-pressurization of the tire:
Probable causes:
- Poorly balanced compressor weight
- Weight gauge or valve issue
- Incorrect mounting on the edge and voluntary over-pressurization when seating the tire on the edge

b. Zipper Disaster:
When a tire has been underinflated for the load, it may become damaged internally. Driving on underinflated tires can lead to the zipper rupture, which is a very dangerous tire condition. Drivers should use extreme caution in handling a tire that has a zipper rupture. It is known that if tire inflation pressure becomes less than 80 percent of the fleet standard, that the driver should deflate the tire by removing the valve core and then removing the tire and wheel rim assembly from the vehicle. When this zipper effect occurs, it can result in prompt, critical air loss. The tire may have a forceful projectile-like eruption of pieces of the tire. These scenarios are extremely dangerous.

Probable causes:
- Deterioration of the envelope uncovering the plys or the belts of the tire to contagion via air or moisture
- Mechanical effect that harms the tire's structure
- Driving with under-pressurized tires below 80 percent of the suggested weight
- Driving with over-pressurized tires

- Overloading of the trailer, which causes extreme stress on the tires
- Loss of mechanical properties because of hotness, pyrolysis, or thermo-oxidation
- Significant remains wear and tire tread
- Design flaw in the weave of the cord of the tire

c.   Tire Demounting:

Tire demounting is another hazard that is a known problem in the industry. This occurs when the tire demounts from the edge of the rim with resulting air and gasses from inside the tire causing a severe eruption.

Probable causes:

- Mechanical effect with high force on the edge of the tire
- Abnormal wear on the edge of the rim
- Deformation of the edge or one of its parts after overheating
- Improper mounting of the tire onto the rim
- Incompatible parts of the edge with a multipiece edge
- Dimensional or other incompatibilities of the edge and tire

d.   Tires in Poor Condition or with Structural Defects:

Tire wear conditions can create risky and hazardous driving conditions for the operator of a large truck or motor carrier. The tire, for whatever reason, develops a defect from wear and becomes hazardous. The tire may be too weak to withstand ordinary inflation pressure.

One of the more common causes of tire wear is under-inflation of the tire due to the driver failing to check tire pressures on a daily basis. When a tire is underinflated by as little as six pounds, it can cause a problem with the operation of the tractor-trailer on the roadway and lead to shifting of the vehicle back and forth across the highway. The driver can lose control, which can lead to the inability to maintain the appropriate lane of travel. The overinflated truck tire leads to a stiffer ride for the driver. When the truck comes across potholes and other known defects in the highway, the tractor-trailer may shift rapidly because of the stiff tire and over-inflation. Daily inspection of tire pressures is absolutely necessary.

Tread separation is another dangerous condition that may make the treads of the tire separate and rapidly cause the tire to explode or blow out. Many trucking companies utilize retread or recapped tires. The use of the recapped or retreaded tires is to save money by avoiding the purchase and cost of new tread tires. While legal, retread tires are known to be dangerous and often cause accidents. Safe motor carriers tend to purchase new tires and new equipment rather than use parts that are known to have defects. Obviously, retreads are less expensive than a new tire. Looking strictly from a safety perspective, it would be in the best interests of all motorists on the roadways to require motor carriers to use only new tires.

Improper Inflation
Tire industry studies have demonstrated that the improper under-inflation of tires will make the tire much more vault vulnerable to wear and tear. On an eighteen-wheeler, the under-inflation of one tire may cause damage to adjacent tires or tires that are in front or in back of the underinflated tire, since that tire is not carrying its necessary support for the entire frame. The under-inflation of tires can lead to overheating and tire failure. Many accidents are related to tires that either deflate or inflate rapidly due to inflation issues. Almost all of these inflation issues are preventable by simply performing the daily tire inspection and pressure check. Appropriate inflation will create a longer life of tires. Truck drivers should be required to write down the tire pressures of each pre-trip inspection in

order to determine whether or not they have actually checked the tire pressures.

High temperature in a tire can lead to significant tire blow-outs and explosions. Tires are known to flex and change structure as they move down the road, causing pressure and force on the rubber, elastic, and steel internal strings of the manufactured tire. Tire wear is a known consequence of contact between the tire and the street. When a tire becomes hot and over-expands, a significant point of contact with the street occurs. This problem creates an uneven contact between the tire and the pavement. When the tire comes in contact with road defects, it can easily blow out and explode. Again, most of this can be avoided by simple pre-trip daily inspections.

Safety Measures

Many manufacturers of automobiles now have automatic sensors built into the valves of the tires. The driver of the automobile can determine whether a tire is overinflated or underinflated by getting a dashboard warning that informs the driver to stop the vehicle to change the pressure of a particular tire. Regulations should be passed to require the mandatory use of these computerized sensors for all large trucks and tractor-trailers in order to prevent these highly frequent accidents from occurring.

Assuming that the manufacturers of tractors for tractor-trailers will resist and fight spending additional monies on computerized safety centers for tire inflation, appropriate safety measures should be implemented to make sure the driver has a consistent awareness of the dangers of tires. The truck driver should be supplied with accurate tire gauges for tire pressure. The truck driver should not be penalized for stopping to replace tires or for checking the tires on a daily basis and notifying the motor carrier of the need for replacement.

The motor carrier should create and implement a training system for the truck drivers to train them to be aware of recognized and known problems with trucks and to look for certain conditions, like the following:

1. Alternate lug wear
2. Both shoulder wear
3. Brake skid
4. Spotty wear
5. Cupping and scalloping
6. Diagonal wear
7. Erosion wear
8. Feather edge wear
9. Heel/toe wear
10. One-sided wear
11. Rib punch
12. Shoulder scrubbing
13. Shoulder step

Truck drivers should be appropriately trained to look for all of the above issues that can occur with a tire. The truck drivers should learn how to take their hand and rub it across the tread and silo sidewalls to look for problems like spots that are not level, cuts, shoulder wear, swelling, sidewall weakness, tread depth, and other visible and noticeable problems that occur just prior to tire blowouts. The driver can then take the truck to the nearest maintenance and repair station to have the tire replaced. This will help avoid accidents.

Pre-trip inspection and the adherence to the FMCSR inspection protocols must be methodically following by truck drivers. The motor carrier should require truck drivers to complete the following inspection before each and every trip.

- Inspect tires before the driver commences operation
- Check tires for swelling, over-inflation, under-inflation, and similar problems.

- Measure tread depth on a weekly basis and check for tires with known tread problems on a daily basis
- Inspect for tire valve problems
- Perform visual and hand inspections of both sides of the tires, meaning on the outside and then by using a board with wheels to lay on their back and inspect the inside portions of the tires

Formal rules of driver training on how to avoid an accident should be taught, trained, and implemented through appropriate classroom and video training. Comprehensive written testing should follow all training. Truck drivers should be taught the following skills to prevent accidents after a tire blowout:

- Never hit the brake since it will cause the vehicle to pull forcefully in one direction or another
- Learn to accelerate the motor vehicle in order to reduce side force
- Use the appropriate ten o'clock and two o'clock grip to the steering wheel and maintain a strong, firm grip on the steering wheel to avoid abrupt lane changes.
- Steer in the opposite direction of the pull of the tractor-trailer
- Use driving simulation devices and programs to learn how to deal with the adverse force caused by the blowout
- Get the vehicle in control and then slowly reduce speed and turn flashers on to warn other drivers of the hazard nearby
- Pull the tractor-trailer over to a safe side road or onto the side of the roadway that is not traveled, stop, and then put safety triangles, cones, and flashers on to warn of the impending hazard and danger.

Antilock Brakes

Trucking manufacturers and motor carriers should mandate that all trucks and tractor-trailers are equipped with antilock brakes. This will help the truck driver stop more quickly. The truck driver still needs to drive within a safe and appropriate speed to be able to stop the tractor-trailer quickly when loaded heavily. Antilock brakes are especially useful in wet road conditions. All trucks, semis, tractor-trailers, and passenger cars should be equipped with antilock brakes.

Cab Safety

Truck cabs are often not required to meet the same safety standards as passenger cars. They should have three-point belts or air bags installed. It is vital to ensure driver and passenger safety.

Shifting of Weight During Transportation

The shifting of cargo and weight is another significant problem with the transportation industry and tractor-trailers in general. One of the most important training rules for drivers is to follow the appropriate loading regulations so that shifting of cargo does not occur during transportation. An improperly loaded truck is generally defined as a truck that has been overloaded by weight or bulk. Many accidents are caused by the truck driver that fails to properly load and secure the cargo. A secondary problem arises when the truck driver fails to check that another independent contractor or customer has properly loaded the cargo into the trailer and secured it appropriately.

There are many circumstances where cargo falls off flatbed trailers and causes death and injury to motorists. There are many other circumstances where tractor-trailers have a shift of weight and cargo during transport, causing the tractor-trailer to veer across lanes of travel or tip over. These circumstances are known and foreseeable. Thus, they are regulated under the FMCSR.

Part 393.100 of the FMCSR addresses protection against shifting or falling cargo. The rules in that particular regulation are applicable to trucks, trailers, and pulled trailers. The requirements are stringent and state that each commercial motor vehicle must, when transporting cargo on public roads, be loaded and equipped, and the cargo secured, in accordance with this subpart to prevent the cargo from leaking, spilling, blowing, or falling from the motor vehicle. Cargo must be contained, immobilized, or secured in accordance with this subpart to prevent shifting upon or within the vehicle to such an extent that the vehicle's stability or maneuverability is adversely affected.

Part 393.102 provides for minimum performance criteria for cargo securement devices and systems. That section of the regulation addresses the breaking strength performance criteria. It also describes working-load limits. The regulation addresses performance criteria for devices to prevent vertical movement of loads that are not contained within the structure of the vehicle.

The regulation provides that securement systems must provide a downward force equivalent to at least 20 percent of the weight of the article of the cargo if the article is not fully contained within the structure of the vehicle.

The regulation addresses the means of securing articles of cargo, including immobilization, such that cargo cannot shift or tip to the extent that the vehicle's instability or maneuverability is adversely affected.

The regulation addresses transportation of cargo in a sided vehicle with side walls. The sided vehicle or trailer walls must be built of adequate strength, such that each article of cargo within the vehicle is in contact with or sufficiently close to the wall or other articles so that the load cannot shift or tip to the extent that the vehicle's stability or maneuverability is adversely affected. The cargo must be secured in accordance with the applicable requirements of Parts 393.104 through Part 393.136 of the FMCSR.

There is a prohibition on the use of damaged securement devices. The regulation requires that drivers and motor carriers address vehicle structures and anchor points, as well as materials for dunnage, chalks, cradles, shoring bars, or for blocking and bracing, and the materials must not have damage or defects that would compromise the effectiveness of the securement system.

The regulations under the FMCSR use a table that is identified as part 393.108 on working and load limits. Truck drivers must be trained and supervised in order to be able to understand the specific chart limits for each load that they transport across the United States. They are complicated and difficult to understand. Failure to comprehend these charts and principles leads to thousands of accidents every year.

When a load is not secured properly by the truck driver's company, or is overweight, it causes the driver to have a limited or minimized ability to drive safely. The minute that the load shifts due to improper loading or overweight conditions, the likelihood of an accident occurring increases.

According to the IIHS, loaded trailers require 20 percent to 40 percent more time to stop as compared to cars. This finding represents clear evidence that the heavier the truck is, the higher the chance of weight shifting during transit. Thus, the likelihood of an accident increases.

The physics related to the mass, acceleration, and force of the tractor-trailer with a full load change as the weight or mass increases. The weight of an average empty tractor-trailer is approximately thirty thousand pounds while that of a full truck averages fifty thousand pounds. Many tractor-trailers with fully loaded cargo reach eighty thousand pounds.

When a tractor-trailer is loaded with excessive cargo, it has an effect on the vehicle's stability. This simultaneously creates problems for the tractor-trailer to maintain a single lane of travel. Shifting of weight will cause the tractor-trailer to shift lanes. The uneven balances created by the shifting cargo mass and weight can make the truck driver lose control of the tractor-trailer. The shifting may be different in higher wind conditions. All of these factors lead to danger to human life.

The motor carrier itself may be responsible for the overloading of the truck and trailer. At times, it is the driver who has chosen to overload the tractor-trailer. In other circumstances, it may be a third-party shipper or loading company that may inappropriately overload the trailer. In all circumstances where an accident occurs, one or all of these parties may be responsible for the accident.

Once an accident occurs due to improper loading or inappropriate securement of the cargo, the lawyer representing an injured party will be investigating to determine which person or entity was responsible for the improper loading or securement. This will take review and discovery of substantial records from all persons and entities involved. Defense lawyers will attempt to withhold as much information as possible. Many times, the trucking company will fail to give their lawyer the appropriate information and the lawyer may be unaware that the information exists. Appropriate deposition of witnesses leads to disclosure that the evidence still exists. Developing this information is difficult and time-consuming. It takes intense study of obscure documents with comparison of related transportation dock documents, such as bills of lading and contracts of delivery and pickup, to determine who was ultimately responsible for the improper loading.

The FMCSA by itself cannot provide all of the appropriate enforcement that is necessary. Funds are limited.

Self-regulation by the industry is required in order to make the transportation industry safer. Utilizing computer software programs and satellite tracking programs, combined with regular monitoring by the motor carrier, will improve safety.

Improper Trailer Attachment

The proper attachment of trailers to trucks, tractors, and other motor vehicles is a major reason for motor vehicle accidents. A research study that was conducted by a national insurance agency established that approximately 70 percent of trailer managers did not know there was an appropriate protocol on how to connect, hitch, and pull the trailers appropriately. The same study discovered that individuals who leased trailers or trucks were frequently not provided appropriate training about the attachment of trailers to the truck or tractor or how to connect the lighting and other braking equipment.

In an alternate study in 2007, the NHTSA found that drivers towing trailers caused in excess of fifty-three thousand trailer accidents, which led to approximately twenty-one thousand injuries and four hundred fifty deaths.

Whenever a trailer detaches from the vehicle towing it, the trailer becomes a deadly uncontrolled instrument of injury and destruction. Serious injuries and wrongful deaths occur due to improper training of drivers. Additional training, including comprehensive testing to determine if drivers really understand how to appropriately attach a trailer, is necessary to prevent further injuries.

Trailers become detached and disconnected from the towing motor vehicle for a variety of reasons, some of which are below.

- Mechanical failure
- Operator behavior where a driver is traveling too fast for the weight and condition of the trailer with its load

- Failure to provide appropriate warnings and lighting, including brake lights and turn signs that are not working on the trailer
- Switch failures
- Metallurgical or component failures from improper manufacture of the equipment
- Failure to utilize an appropriate safety chain to secure the trailer to the truck or motor vehicle
- Lack of proper maintenance and repair on the trailer and connective devices
- Improper operation of the truck or motor vehicle while towing a trailer
- Failure to train the driver/operator with appropriate safety skills
- Failure to provide appropriate safety harnesses, chains, and connective equipment
- Failure to have appropriate electrical and lighting connections with electrical shorts, burned-out lights, and other failures regarding provision of electricity to the lights
- Fast and abrupt stopping of a heavy load without appropriate braking, causing the trailer to push the truck into stopped traffic
- Inappropriate compliance with the FMCSR and applicable state and federal laws, ordinance, statutes, and regulations
- Inappropriate compliance with weight limitations of the trailer or overloading

Many accidents are caused by improperly trained operators who do not understand how to appropriately attach the trailers and their connective devices. Many more accidents are caused by pulling overloaded trailers that have shifting cargo and weight. These improperly loaded trailers cause the tractors and trucks to veer from lane to lane, where they collide with other vehicles, causing injury and death. Almost all of these accidents can be prevented through proper supervision and training. Drivers towing trailers must understand the physics involved with pulling trailers. They must understand the load requirements of the FMCSR. Compliance with industry standards and the minimum standards set forth by the FMCSR will help alleviate thousands of accidents a year. It is recommended that the federal regulations be strengthened and monitored to a much more stringent set of standards. Monitoring of the trucking industry should be increased to a point where compliance is the norm.

6

CAUSES OF TRUCK ACCIDENTS

THE CAUSE OF truck accidents is a perplexing study that requires evaluation of a number of criteria and variables. Those will be discussed below. The first issue is the qualifications of the driver. Part 391.11 from the FMCSR requires that all drivers be properly qualified before operating a truck or tractor-trailer. Part 391.23 requires investigations and background checks of the drivers, which includes obtaining a three-year driving history with actual responses from past employers.

Many trucking companies simply ask for a copy of the Commercial Driver's License (CDL) and then run a quick check. The driver starts driving without a road test and the unqualified driver begins on their merry way down the highway. The FMCSA has addressed the fact that having a CDL does not make the truck driver qualified. Companies will have the driver sign a certification sheet certifying that they are familiar with the FMCSR Safety Handbook and believe they have complied with the law. They have not. It requires much more than looking at the CDL and having the driver sign a sheet of paper stating he has read and is familiar with the FMCSR. This concept is ludicrous.

The FMCSR Safety Handbook is an extremely regulatory book based on the Code of Federal Regulations. It is written by lawyers and legislators. Many truck drivers cannot answer basic questions asked about the book's regulatory requirements and will admit they have never read it. More importantly, many will admit they do not understand the requirements of the book. This is why they have management editions of the safety regulations in order to have safety directors learn the regulations and then implement a safety protocol to teach the meaning of each regulation in a way that can be understood and comprehended by the average truck driver.

Huge trucks, e.g., tankers, tractor-trailers, semis, or eighteen-wheelers, are significantly larger in size than the smaller passenger vehicles, pickups, and SUVs traveling the nation's streets, highways, and turnpikes. If a highway is a faster roadway with a higher speed limit, the mistakes of the truck driver can be much more significant due to the reduction in perception and reaction time of not only the truck driver, but also the operator of the passenger vehicle. A small mistake may lead to a huge catastrophe that could have been prevented at a slower speed.

Most truck drivers comprehend the dangers they confront on the roadway and take safeguards to drive safely and competently. Notwithstanding the safe and careful drivers, there are truck drivers who will not follow the rules and do whatever it takes to get to the scheduled delivery on time so they are not penalized monetarily for a late delivery. Truck driver errors are ordinarily created by driver fatigue, failing to follow the FMCSR safety regulations, failure to properly secure a load, driving while on methamphetamine and other stimulants, driving while intoxicated, or overloading the trailer per regulations.

Drivers who are not properly supervised, dispatched, and trained lead to accidents and death. Under the FMCSR, a truck driver must be properly qualified and trained in order to be able to operate the large trucks and tractor-trailers. This requires having a road test to prove that the driver has sufficient hazard perception skills so as not to be a danger on the road. Poorly trained drivers lead to accidents. Failure to administer comprehensive written tests to drivers after training to determine how much he or she understood from the training process is a major flaw with many smaller motor carriers. They give the driver a FMCSR regulation book and have him sign a document saying he has read it, but no training is provided. Many drivers are unable to understand many of the regulations due to a fundamental system flaw—lack of training. Motor carriers that follow the rules use classroom training and videotape presentations to teach drivers about hazards. After the training, they conduct tests to determine the proficiency and knowledge of the driver. This is not a mandatory system so many smaller companies with ten trucks and under never provide any knowledge to the drivers. When the driver is out on the highways, they cause accidents.

Brakes: At 55 mph, a passenger vehicle can normally stop inside 130 to 140 feet. In contrast, a fully loaded big rig can take 190 to 200 feet of stopping distance to reach a final resting point. An overloaded semi with poorly maintained brakes may take four hundred to five hundred feet or longer to reach a complete stop. The truck driver does not realize that the poorly maintained brakes and overloaded vehicle will not stop as fast as a properly maintained and loaded vehicle. This leads to the inability to stop, collision with a passenger car, and severe injury and death to the occupants of the smaller vehicle.

Increasing speed: Truck drivers often speed down hills and mountains, where they can become instruments of destruction. This is why many states have truck ramps that allow the speeding and out of control tractor-trailer to drive on a long ramp that takes it uphill to stop it from building a velocity that is unsafe for everyone. In Wyoming, they have developed large types of rubber bands that catch the semis, then expand and slow their rate of acceleration as a method to avoid someone dying.

Visibility and Blind Spots: Tractor-trailers have huge blind spots in the back, on both sides, and in proximity to the tractor near the immediate rear of the driver's seat on either side of the tractor. These blind spots are known to the truck driver, but not always to the approaching or passing motorist. Blind spots can be from a few feet to as much one hundred to two hundred feet, depending on the length of the trailer or tandem trailer. The blind spots are on the sides, in the back, and in the front of the tractor cab. Oftentimes, drivers of these larger vehicles miss pedestrians, bicyclists, and animals that are outside of their visible area of sight and these innocents are injured or killed.

Mobility: Big trucks require additional room to make turns. Drivers frequently move to the left to make a right turn. Likewise, on multipath streets, truckers will veer toward the center path in light of the fact that it provides additional room for completion of their turn. Passenger vehicle drivers need to stay as far away from a turning tractor-trailer as humanly possible in order to avoid injury.

Another leading cause is the pay-by-mile to deliver-on-time system. The truck company and their drivers dispatch without determining actual driving time of the driver. A good company will not dispatch until they know the time a driver has left to drive without violating the FMCSR. The drivers only know they get paid if they are on time and if they arrive late, the motor carrier docks their pay, reprimands them for an untimely delivery, and in some cases, fires them. This type of system is a self-fulfilling prophecy. The obvious becomes true: the driver is dispatched to drive over the required hours, becomes tired and fatigued, and causes a catastrophe. In order to keep jobs, drivers push themselves to the limit and violate the maximum hours rules. The system does not work well for truck drivers or the people they injure and kill in passenger cars.

In many cases the truck driver or motor carrier or both are to blame for the accidents. In some, the fault lies with the passenger car, but for the most part, the truck driver is to blame. Many truck drivers are concerned with loss of income, reprimands, and potential termination for late deliveries so they are taught to be quiet about problems. They all know a fellow driver who took the time to complain about a safety issue and then immediately was fired. Some of the larger trucking companies know the rules. They teach in classroom settings and test for comprehension. Those safer companies will track hours of their drivers. When a driver is short of hours, he is not dispatched for a load that will violate the maximum hours rules. Unfortunately, safely operated trucking companies are few and far between. In a safe company, the truck driver is allowed to report a safety problem without fear of being fired or reprimanded. The truck driver in a safe company learns the rules, follows the procedures, and plays the game according to the book.

The causes of truck driver errors, as discussed, are many. Education, training, supervision, and monitoring of the education process of the truck drivers in order to comply with the FMCSR will lead to fewer accidents and deaths. Manufacturers of large trucks and tractor-trailers must be forced by mandatory regulation to add safety devices to these large instruments of death and destruction. Motor carriers must institute and follow disciplinary policies, including the Rule of 3, which is the industry standard of care. This is the three-strike rule and you are out. This relates to giving a driver three chances before final termination. But simply creating safety policies is not enough. The policy and disciplinary process must be fully implemented, followed, taught, analyzed, and carried through to its end means in order to have any true effect on society.

Bad truck drivers need to be eliminated. Motor carriers that have good truck drivers need to be able to recognize which bad drivers are not worthy of hiring. The bad truck drivers who go through a system of rehabilitation can be retrained and retested. If proven worthy of a second chance, then they can be placed back on the nation's highways. There is no reason to keep a truck driver who continuously violates the FMCSR and state statutes and regulations, which are designed to promote safety to the motoring public.

As each new technology becomes available, the government must study the cost-benefit analysis for each particular product. For those products that have a reasonable cost with a high promotion of safety, regulation should require their use on all old and new trucks and tractor-trailers.

Education of truck drivers must be done at the very minimum on a quarterly basis. The truck drivers must attend continuing education classes, like attorneys, doctors, and other business professionals so that they learn the changes in the laws and how to comply with the laws. Drivers must be comprehensively tested in a written format to determine whether they are safe to operate a large truck. If a truck driver cannot show a basic level of comprehension of the information studied in the test then the government should prevent that truck driver from driving. Those types of truck drivers need to get a different occupation that does not affect public safety.

Blind Spots

Truckers and blind spots go hand in hand. Blind spots are areas where the truck driver cannot see around the truck. The California driver handbook has a section on blind spots for vehicles. It diagrams the actual areas where truckers may have blind spots. These include areas immediately behind the tractor-trailer. They include the areas that are in a triangle going backward from where the driver can see out the front window of the cab and angle backward behind and to the side of the cab. The driver cannot see at a certain angle to the back, on either side of the semi. There are also blind spots in the area that is immediately to the right of the passenger side of the front cab and immediately in front of the truck. Many accidents occur because of the truck driver's failure to recognize that there may be cars in these blind spots. Operators of cars may unknowingly stay in a truck's blind spots because of their fear to pass the larger, more dangerous tractor-trailer.

The industry has attempted to create large mirrors to try to eliminate the blind spots. The problem is that the mirrors cannot completely eliminate the blind spots. This is why truck drivers must be exceptionally careful when changing lanes, and should refrain from accelerating or decelerating too quickly.

The way a truck is constructed can also cause blind spots. Support pillars in the cab are usually very wide to protect the driver from rollover accidents. The width of these pillars creates additional blind spots for the truck driver.

Part 393.80 of the FMCSR describes the requirements for rear-vision mirrors. It requires that every bus, truck, and tractor-trailer be equipped with two rear-vision mirrors, one at each side, firmly attached to the outside of the motor vehicle, and so located as to reflect to the driver a view of the highway to the rear along both sides of the vehicle. All such regulated rear-vision mirrors and the replacements shall meet, at a minimum, the requirements of FMVSS No. 111 (49 CFR 571.11). The DOT and the FMCSA recognized this need quite some time ago. Newer inventions, like rear-vision and side-vision cameras, should be placed in all tractor-trailers and large trucks so that the truck driver has a series of viewing screens to see the entire surrounding area of the tractor-trailer, including the front, the sides, and behind the vehicle. This would help to eliminate an enormous amount of accidents.

Driving a large truck in reverse is considered to be one of the most difficult challenges for a truck driver because of the size of the truck and the many blind spots. Pedestrians can be killed when a truck driver is backing up and fails to see them. Installing cameras in the rear of the truck would eliminate those accidents. Approximately eight hundred forty thousand accidents in the United States are caused annually due to blind spots. These types of accidents lead to approximately three hundred deaths every year.

The most common blind spot is the rear quarter blind spot. This is when the driver cannot see both sides of the area toward the rear of the vehicle. The most common accident due to blind spots takes place while drivers change lanes.

Tractor Design Factors to Eliminate Blind Spots
- The design of these large vehicles contributes a great deal to the inability of the truck drivers to see all around the truck. The vehicles can be designed in such a way that would allow the blind spots to be eliminated. This includes substantial mirrors, viewing cameras and television monitors for the front, sides, and back of the tractor-trailer or large trucks.
- The technology is presently available in passenger cars. The motor carrier industry and the manufacturers of the tractor-trailers are hesitant to implement the new camera and sonar technology because of the cost. Regulations must be implemented to require the new technology to be mandatory on newly built trucks. Similar regulations should require that this newer technology be retrofitted into older trucks and tractor-trailers.

The main causes of truck driver errors include fatigue, alcohol use, drug use, texting on a cellular phone or device, talking on a cellular phone or even a hands-free cellular phone or device, and failing to be properly trained in all aspects of safe-driving skills. The following chapters will discuss in-depth the main causes of driver error, and will provide the reader with a better understanding of why large trucks kill humans, whether they are pedestrians, bicyclists, motorcyclists, passenger car drivers, or operators of other smaller vehicles.

Truck Drivers and Bad Weather—A Deadly Combination
Truck drivers that drive in bad weather are completely disregarding safety and the FMCSR. Rain, snow, mist, ice, and other weather factors like high winds create dangerous situations. The intelligent truck driver will recognize and anticipate ahead of time that the truck speed should be reduced and/or that the truck should be completely taken out of service and discontinued until the weather improves. Unfortunately, many truck drivers fail to heed the rules of the FMCSR regarding the need for discontinuance of service.

Hazardous conditions require extreme caution. Under part 392.14 of the FMCSR, it requires that extreme caution in the operation of a commercial motor vehicle shall be exercised when hazardous conditions, such as those caused by snow, ice, sleet, fog, mist, rain, dust, or smoke, adversely affect visibility or traction. Speed shall be reduced when such conditions exist. If conditions become sufficiently dangerous, the operation of the commercial motor vehicle shall be discontinued and shall not be resumed until the commercial motor vehicle can be safely operated. This rule is often misunderstood. It means that the truck driver **shall** discontinue operation of the tractor-trailer in bad and extreme conditions and not resume until the conditions have dissipated. It is one of the least followed rules in the FMCSR.

Any time bad weather exists, it is presumed that the roads will become slippery and dangerous. Common sense tells all drivers that misty and icy roads can be extremely dangerous. Commercial motor vehicles need to be more aware of this rule because of the mass and size of their vehicle. The force of the trailer increases as it loses control, and starts to slip and slide across bad roads. A slippery surface can cause a tractor-trailer to turn in a ninety degree angle, where it can take out all other cars surrounding it. Once the tractor-trailer starts into a spin or other type of loss of control, the truck driver is completely unable to prevent an accident. At that moment, the heavier the load, the worse the situation will be. Most truck drivers fail to take into consideration the weight of their load and when they fail to do so, they are likely to cause misery and death.

The average truck driver or operator has a larger duty to control the tractor-trailer because of this particular regulation. It does not give the driver very much discretion. This regulation generally requires the driver to heed the regulation by reducing speed and when bad enough, the driver must cease operations. Whenever bad weather is present and a truck driver has been involved in the accident, it is likely the truck driver's fault for not ceasing and discontinuing operation of the tractor-trailer. The driver could simply pull over to the side of the road and put lights on or find a side road to pull off on. Drivers can look for truck stops and other parking lot areas where the truck can safely wait for the storm to pass.

In states with high wind levels like Kansas, Indiana, Illinois, and others, news stories routinely display tractor-trailers that have been overturned by high winds. Many of these tractor-trailers end up smashing into motorists by being too close to them. Discontinuation of service until the high winds are reduced would prevent the tractor-trailer from overturning. The driver does not want to stop because of the fact that he will lose compensation and may likely be repri-manded or fired for stopping.

An inherent problem with bad weather is maneuvering the long tractor-trailer along the highways without having it veer back and forth across the roadway. Slippery surfaces and extreme wind can cause the vehicle to fail to stay in its own lane of travel. The truck is forced into vehicles that are near its sides or worse, into oncoming traffic. Once a tractor-trailer loses control, the motorist near that tractor-trailer needs to stay as far away from the tractor-trailer as possible until it stops its forward or sideward forceful movement. This is one of the reasons why operators of cars should stay as far away from tractor-trailers as possible.

Untrained or overconfident truck drivers make many poor decisions during storm conditions. Truck drivers should be wary of driving in bad weather conditions. Truck drivers have an obligation to follow this regulation and reduce speed. There are many errors that truck drivers make in bad weather conditions that lead to fatal accidents. Some are:

- Failing to discontinue operation and pull off the trave-led roadway
- Failing to operate at a reduced speed for the wet, windy, and low visibility conditions
- Continuing to operate in foggy conditions of almost zero visibility
- Driving on snow and black ice that has not been treated
- Operating too fast for unknown road conditions
- Operating at a speed that will lose traction and cause the vehicle to go into a skid or slide
- Driving without appropriate lights in low visibility nighttime conditions

- Driving in high wind conditions that could cause the trailer to catch the wind and make the tractor-trailer overturn
- Driving too fast in icy and snowy conditions too close behind traffic in front of the driver
- Losing control of the tractor-trailer by losing traction and fishtailing
- Failing to anticipate that additional braking time is necessary
- Failing to anticipate that additional perception and reaction time is necessary due to the inability to stop quickly

Motor carriers must use classroom, videotape, and teacher orientation training to train truck drivers about this particular regulation and the fact that the tractor-trailer will have poor handling characteristics in bad weather conditions. The truck driver needs to be taught that the driver's perception and reaction times are adversely affected in bad weather conditions. The truck driver must learn that braking is much more difficult in bad weather conditions, especially with a heavy load. The truck driver needs to understand how a tractor-trailer can lose traction and then do a sideways fishtail across the highway or skid off the highway entirely. Only appropriate training and supervision will eliminate truck drivers who ignore this mandatory regulation about extreme weather conditions.

7

DRUG AND ALCOHOL
USE AS LEADING CAUSES OF
ERRORS

O NE CAUSE OF truck accidents that is widespread and
increasing in the United States is truck drivers driving under the influence of alcohol. In 2004, an astounding
number of driving under the influence (DUI) accidents were
recorded. Another leading cause of truck accidents is drivers'
use of stimulants and other drugs to fight fatigue. The use of
prescribed and illegal drugs by truck drivers is on the rise.
In order to drive longer hours with short periods of sleep,
truck drivers may turn to stimulants like methamphetamine,
ice, crystal, speed, Dexedrine, Ritalin, Adderall, and a host
of other stimulants. These drugs can be readily purchased at
drug stops tired drivers are known to frequent. Some drivers
may turn to cocaine and crack. All of these drugs have a mind-
altering effect on the human body. They cause hallucina-
tions, breaks in thought patterns, and many other side effects.
Drivers may feel confident that they can drive another five
hundred miles, when in reality they should be pulling over to
rest in their sleeper or at a motel.

Some drivers may choose to take cannabis, commonly
known as pot, weed, or grass. Different varieties of marijuana

have different effects on the driver. Drivers seeking marijuana will look for the type that gives them a talkative, speeding feeling rather than the type that makes them slow down. Marijuana will make a person feel very relaxed and laid back. Intake impairs concentration, which causes the person to be unable to perform complex tasks due to extreme and sudden fatigue. The long-term effects of using marijuana include paranoia and heart problems, as well as breathing and respiratory problems, which have a coincidental relationship to sleep and fatigue. One study in 1999 found that marijuana was present in 4 percent of drivers in accidents. That figure rose to 12 percent in 2010.

Ecstasy or MDMA comes in pill form. When taken, the driver may feel super levels of energy. The mind-altering effects of this type of stimulant will wreak havoc on the truck driver's ability to concentrate. It can and will lead to accidents and catastrophe.

Prescription medications may be as bad as street drugs. Truck drivers who have back pain from long periods of sitting may end up taking Lortab, Percocet, Norco, and other similar pain medications. These prescriptions are easy to get. With more and more prescriptions for pain medications being written by liberal doctors, known as script doctors, the truck driver may be able to easily obtain these legal drugs to drive. The problem is that most of these medications have warnings and adverse risk statements that indicate the patient should not drive while taking the medication. These types of medications will reduce a driver's thought process and create longer perception and reaction time to hazards on the road. Even two to three seconds may be enough of a difference to result in an accident.

Prescription painkillers are known to be addictive. Their effects worsen with alcohol use. They slow down the respiratory system and the truck driver's reaction time becomes slower, ultimately resulting in the inability to safely drive a large tractor-trailer.

Truck drivers who suffer from depression or anxiety disorders should have regular screenings for medical clearance. Some of the medications prescribed for depression and anxiety, like Prozac, Wellbutrin, Zoloft, Effexor, Pristiq, Cymbalta, Trazadone, Remeron, Lexapro, Celexa, and Paxil, affect the serotonin and dopamine levels in the brain. These medications all provide warnings to the user regarding adverse effects of driving or operating heavy machinery while using the medications. It is known that they will slow down the perception and reaction time of the driver.

Anti-anxiety medications like Valium and Xanax are no better. They have severe reductions on the respiratory and metabolic rates of the patient. In turn, they reduce the driver's ability to perceive and react to hazards and dangers on the road.

With antidepressants and anti-anxiety medications, the risk that follows consumption of the prescribed medication is a risk of momentary pauses and sleep while driving. Long driving hours, combined with ingesting unsafe prescription medications, can lead to microsleep moments, where a driver dozes off for a second or two.

The dangers of illegal and prescribed drugs are a known hazard. Truck companies are required to drug test drivers upon hire and many do so at random intervals during a year. The FMCSR requires both drug and alcohol tests immediately after an accident. Why? Because the use of drugs and alcohol by truck drivers is widely known in the industry. The FMCSR was partially designed to detect and prevent addicted drivers from driving large trucks.

Many states have now instituted statutes, laws, and ordinances that make it illegal for a driver to drive while on a prescription medication that contains a manufacturer's warning not to drive. At least twelve states have made it illegal to drive if a certain amount of a prescribed drug is found in a person's blood. Some of the states are Arizona, Minnesota, and Wisconsin. Every year, more and more states are adding new laws to make driving while intoxicated on prescription drugs an illegal offense punishable with jail time and fines. The FMCSA and most state governments are aware that driving on certain types of mind-altering prescription drugs is known to impair driving skills, judgment, reaction time, and perception time. Random monthly drug testing of drivers of large trucks through a simple urine test will eliminate many truck related accidents.

Some studies in the United States have identified driver intoxication rates as high as 40 percent. Law officials and the FMCSA routinely perform preventability studies of individual crashes with large trucks and calculate the statistical level of intoxication. Motor carriers who do not have proper drug testing schedules and post-accident drug and alcohol testing of drivers can be fined or may lose operating authority under DOT audits.

Recognition and Regulation of Truck Drivers for Drugs and Alcohol

Part 382.301 of the FMCSR discusses pre-employment drug testing. It requires testing a prospective employee who would perform safety-sensitive functions for an employer. The employee is required to undergo testing for controlled substances prior to being hired, unless certain exceptions apply. The same regulation requires that no employer shall allow a driver to perform safety-sensitive functions unless the employer has received a controlled substance test result verifying a negative test result for that driver.

Part 382.303 of the FMCSR addresses post-accident testing. This section requires the motor carrier to test the driver for alcohol or drugs as soon as practicable following an occurrence involving a commercial motor vehicle operated on a public road in commerce. This requires the employer to test for alcohol where a driver has received a citation within eight hours of the occurrence, and to test for drugs where a driver has received a citation within thirty-two hours of the occurrence. It also requires testing if there has been an accident of bodily injury where any person has to receive medical treatment away from the scene of the accident, where the accident involves loss of human life, and where there is disabling damage as a result of a motor vehicle accident and one of the vehicles is transported away from the scene by a tow truck or other motor vehicle.

These regulations are sometimes confusing to the employer. As a result of that confusion, the FMCSA created a table to guide the employer in the necessary steps to test for drugs or alcohol.

The FMCSR has a table under 382.303 that is useful for determining whether testing is necessary. Motor carriers are able to review that table for a quick reference guide to determine when alcohol or drug testing is mandated by the FMCSR.

Random drug and alcohol testing is controlled by part 382.305 of the FMCSR. This regulatory requirement states that every employer shall comply with the requirements of this section and that every driver shall submit to random alcohol and controlled substance testing as required. The regulation recognizes that the FMCSA administrator's decision to increase or decrease the minimum annual percentage rate for alcohol testing is based on the reported violation rate for the entire industry. All the information used for that determination is drawn from the information supplied by the entire industry pursuant to part 382.403. In order to ensure the reliability of the data, the FMCSA administrator considers the quality and completeness of the reported data and is authorized to obtain additional information or reports from employers. The administrator is authorized to make appropriate modifications in calculating the total industry violation rate. Certain specific guidelines are given to the administrator to increase or decrease the annual percentage-testing rate as necessary.

The same regulation addresses testing for controlled substances based on the reported positive rate for the entire industry. That same information is drawn from the controlled substance management information system reports that are required by part 382.403. The administrator is authorized to look to employers' records and other reported data from information systems in order to make appropriate increases and decreases of the testing requirements.

The Causes of Increased Drug Use in Truck Drivers

The yearly analysis by the FMCSA administrator helps to deter-mine the amount of random drug and alcohol testing that must be carried out as a minimum standard in order for the motor carrier to retain appropriate licensure and authority to oper-ate. The improving economy and growing commerce result in an increase in miles driven by truck drivers. As each additional mile is driven, there is an assumed need for increased regula-tion to protect the motoring public.

Addiction

Drivers who turn to stimulants or other mind-altering medica-tions don't always understand the addictive properties of some of the medications. The drugs that are not as addictive may have a different mechanism of addiction that propels use by the drivers. For example, the driver uses stimulants, which causes a lack of sleep. The longer the stimulant is used, the more tired the driver becomes. To combat the excessive tiredness, the driver may increase the use of the stimulant.

Rehabilitation centers are expensive. Many drivers are self-employed with no health insurance. Those drivers cannot afford to take the time off and many don't have the funds to pay for the rehabilitation centers. Taking time off for rehabilitation would mean losing money to feed their families and possibly losing their contracts with the main carriers they drive for.

Larger carriers that provide health insurance do not set up the necessary pay systems that would allow the addicted driver to take off a month to go through rehab. Without systems in place that reward drivers for recognizing and treating addiction, the recovery process cannot take place. The drivers will continue to drive addicted.

Procedural Flaws in the Motor Carrier Health and Recovery Plans

- Motor carriers do not want to have drivers take off time for recovery. The carriers that set up self-funded ERISA plans do not write health insurance plans allowing for their employees to have sufficient paid time while in treatment. The plans for insurance are underfunded and lack quality health care benefits. The lower the benefits and higher the deductible, the less likely it is that a truck driver will use the available insurance to seek recovery.
- Motor carriers know that roadside inspections are infrequent. They understand that the driver appearing alert will likely prevent law enforcement from seeking a drug or alcohol test until it is too late, after an accident has occurred.
- Some motor carriers completely ignore the mandatory testing requirements and simply place drivers on the road without having certification that the drivers have been adequately and appropriately tested. These types of motor carriers often fail to follow the random testing protocols until an audit from the DOT and FMCSA occurs. The costs associated with random audits may

be a reason for failure to adhere to the required compliance. Every dollar that is not spent on safety precautions creates the potential for an additional dollar of profits. Motor carriers that care little for safety often choose to skip the necessary testing protocols in order to save a buck. If an audit does not occur, they may never be caught. Everyone is aware that the government funding to conduct roadside inspections is insufficient to adequately perform all the inspections and audits necessary to create a safer national system. Unfortunately, self-regulation occurs infrequently.

Procedures to Minimize Intoxicated Truck Drivers on Interstate Commerce

Intoxication of truck drivers due to alcohol, illegal drugs, and prescribed medications is an ongoing and difficult national crisis that is hard to repair. The first and most obvious step is to perform random drug and alcohol testing of all truck drivers at least one time per month on an unspecified basis. Drivers who are addicted can easily predict the period of a normal random urine test. Those addicted drivers are able to control themselves for a period of time and to stop consumption of alcohol and/or drugs for brief periods just prior to the known period of testing. This random monthly testing would have to be done on all drivers for it to have a lasting effect. Presently, many companies perform testing on just a few randomly chosen drivers. The entire fleet is not tested on a monthly basis. Testing the entire fleet each month would allow for much greater safety.

A second step would be for truck companies to provide education to their drivers to help increase driver awareness of the dangers and hazards of operating a commercial motor vehicle while in an intoxicated state.

A third step would be for truck companies to create a compensation system of bonuses for drivers who pass the random drug and alcohol tests over certain periods of time.

The correct answer to fix the system would be to set up a combination procedural system that educates and tests the drivers. The system would compensate and provide bonuses to those drivers who are in compliance with the rules of the FMCSR. Those same drivers who are in compliance could be given fair compensation increases for their safety awareness. Those drivers who are noncompliant could be reprimanded, treated in addiction facilities, and/or terminated. The industry has a standard of care, which is a called the Rule of Three. This is the three-strike rule, which gives a driver three chances before final termination. Strict adherence to the Rule of Three would provide a system of increased compliance. Drivers who do not comply with the rules would be dealt with in a similar way to the DUI laws in most states, which provide punishment ranging from jail time to suspension of a driver's license. The truck driver who continues to operate in an intoxicated state should not be given the privilege of a CDL. A national system of computer recognition could easily flag those drivers so that other motor carriers do not hire them. A driver who then completes an adequate period of sobriety, followed by a certain period of time with adequate random testing, could be put back into service after that driver has established and proven that they no longer are addicted.

8

FATIGUE LEADING TO TRUCK DRIVERS ERRORS

O NE OF THE leading causes of truck accidents is fatigue. Once drivers are too tired to drive, danger rapidly approaches. The federal government recently studied the hours-of-service rules under the Efficacy-of-HOS-Restart-Rule-Report. The link to that report is found at:

http://ntl.bts.gov/lib/51000/51400/51417/Efficacy-of-HOS-Restart-Rule-Report.pdf

This study, which was conducted by the Washington State University Sleep and Performance Research Center for the FMCSR, helped evaluate driver fatigue with different levels of nighttime periods for breaks. The study partially reviewed nighttime drivers and their restart break. The restart break generally leads to the conclusion that adding nighttime sleep for nighttime drivers with the addition of breaks would lead to a safer environment.

The restart is a new cycle for the driver who has been off-duty for thirty-four hours or more. The change in regulations required nighttime drivers to have at least two night periods, which were defined as from 1:00 a.m. to 5:00 a.m., during each restart period in order to allow for enough sleep. The effect of these regulations is that drivers who finish an on-duty cycle of work that ends between 1:00 a.m. and 7:00 p.m. must extend their thirty-four-hour restart break by one or more hours in order to comply with the new rule. Generally, this will help drivers to have less fatigue while driving. It will also help them have fewer attention-span issues.

The government study utilized volunteers who were randomized into a best-case condition, which generally means that they would have daytime wakefulness and nighttime sleep. They compared this to a worst-case condition, where nighttime wakefulness was compared to daytime sleep.

The study consisted of one hundred men and six women between the ages of twenty-four and sixty-nine. The commercial driving experience of the collective study group ranged from less than one year to more than thirty-nine years, with an average or mean of 12.4 years of driving experience. Driver fatigue levels were measured three times per day by means of a Psychomotor Vigilance Test, commonly called the PVT. They then studied the subjective sleepiness scores, as well as lane deviation in duty cycles. The final results indicated that a driver having at least two nighttime periods from 1:00 a.m. until 5:00 a.m. in the restart break will help to mitigate and reduce fatigue.

These government studies lead to a simple conclusion that nighttime drivers are hazardous and dangerous. Giving additional rest periods with days off to compensate for the missed rest will help alleviate the hazards of the truck driver on the open roads.

Many accidents occur during the nighttime hours when all motorists are tired. Even professional truck drivers become tired and fatigued. The change of their normal sleeping patterns can lead to disastrous effects on other drivers. As nighttime comes on, the chances for accidents increase substantially. Changes in alertness create a decreased reaction and perception time. If motor carriers give the drivers sufficient breaks to obtain sleep and rest while simultaneously paying them for their off-duty time, accidents will be decreased.

Some motor carriers change and alternate the schedules of their drivers, which causes them to be unable to have a routine sleep pattern. This alternation of circadian rhythms leads to extremely fatigued drivers, who become dangerous and hazardous to all other motorists.

The problem with fatigue is that it can get to the best of drivers. Even the most experienced drivers can become victim to fatigue. Reports suggest that almost 30 percent of fatal accidents and 15 percent of accidents with injuries are caused by fatigue. Fatigue has been studied and the effects are known. Preventative measures can be taken to eliminate factors that cause drivers to operate on limited periods of rest or sleep. The government determined that additional rules of safety needed to be added for nighttime drivers because of the known dangers of driving at night.

Causes of fatigue

Sleep

- Getting less rest than required. If a driver does not take the appropriate time off between drives and rest, it will lead to and create fatigue and exhaustion.
- Lack of sleep over an extended period of days. By continuing to have only a minimal period of sleep over several days in a row, the exhaustion and fatigue grow exponentially. A driver has a legal obligation to rest and sleep under the FMCSR hours of service regulations. Breaks are needed so that the driver is able to regain an ability to be fresh and rested. When drivers work one hundred hours a week or more to meet the deadlines imposed by the carrier for timely delivery, the driver becomes more and more sleep deprived,

finally reaching a dangerous level of exhaustion that is likely worse than driving while intoxicated. Certainly, driving while intoxicated is illegal and not permissible. Driving while exhausted is similar to driving while intoxicated and should be made illegal. The present FMCSR standards on extended driving hours must be changed to shorter workdays for all drivers.

Work Factors Causing Accidents
- Long driving hours will fatigue a driver and make it dangerous for the driver to continue on the road safely. Long work hours, particularly over more than one day, can cause much more profound exhaustion.
- Nighttime driving is simply dangerous. Driving during the night places an even greater stress on the driver's ability to stay alert and react to or perceive impending hazards and perils. The human body needs sleep and the circadian rhythm studies make that an even greater requirement. Drivers should not be dispatched at night unless they are fully rested.
- Unusual early dispatch times. When motor carriers require a driver to be dispatched late at night or in the early morning hours before sunrise, just to get a load delivered on time, they are making it nearly impossible to have a rested driver. These unusual dispatch times can be avoided altogether by simply having start times that make sense.
- Rapid booking and scheduling for on-time deliveries are hazardous. Trucking companies and freight shippers promise rapid delivery overnight without regard to safety. They have twenty-four hour dispatch services that are picking loads up from all over the country without regard to how many hours a driver has left. This type of booking, while efficient for profit, is a leading

cause of accidents. The government regulators should require mandatory use of on-board time calculation on hours-of-service regulations through a combination of satellite tracking and on-board computer documentation of the hours of each driver. This information can be uploaded by satellite to the dispatcher who would immediate see that the particular truck and driver do not have enough remaining hours to make the delivery safely. In this event, another driver with rest and available hours can pick the load up. The potential for an accident would be lessened.

- Insufficient time to recover from fatigue. Drivers can and should be given sufficient downtime to recover from exhaustion and fatigue. A driver can be required to stop and sleep in the sleeper or a nearby motel until he or she is refreshed.

- Off-duty time means physical work. The FMCSR require the drivers to actually report off-duty time in the calculation of hours. The problem arises from drivers who are busy doing non-driving work like loading and unloading pallets, filling and emptying oil, gas, and chemicals. Many drivers choose to work and say they are off duty in order to make their time schedules. Motor carriers can train the drivers to calculate working time as on duty to follow the safety regulations. The driver has to learn that all work activity counts against available and remaining driving time.

- Poor driving conditions. The FMCSR has a section on hazardous road conditions. The regulation requires the driver to reduce speed in poor driving conditions and, if bad enough, to cease and shut down operation until the driver can safely operate the rig. Some of the conditions are rain, ice, black ice, mist, wet roads, high winds, storms, and other environmental factors that make driving a huge tractor-trailer extremely dangerous.

- Hot and cold climate conditions. Trucks operate differently in cold and hot conditions due to the obvious weather conditions that come with them. Truck drivers must always be prepared for a rapid change in their ability to decrease the speed of the truck. The tractor may have a change in the manner in which it operates differently in cold or hot conditions. Motor carriers should always train the drivers on these variables in order to teach them how to safely avoid accidents.

Time of Day Factors

- Working time versus sleep time. Fatigue and circadian rhythm studies establish that there are better times to work and sleep. Disturbing these naturally occurring rhythms is not helpful to truck drivers. Usually, the body becomes accustomed to a certain time to be up and another to be asleep. Your body has a defined time of day when it requires rest and sleep. Much of this is from the timing of the sun and moon. Your body will work on a twenty-four-hour clock. When the sun goes down, your body will respond appropriately by letting your internal clock begin to prepare for rest and sleep. Likewise, after a normal pattern of sleep, when the sun rises, your body has a natural need to wake up. At the point when the sun goes down, your body responds by planning for slumber. When twelve noon arrives, your body will naturally be altered to another state with hormones. In some societies, this is called the siesta timeframe. In other words, if a driver has been driving for a prolonged period of time, then a short off-duty period of rest in the early afternoon will help keep the driver alert. Some people are able to take short naps, while others are unable to take the time to rest. After twelve noon, your "body clock" may change your body temperature, your ability to be alert, or make other changes that affect overall alertness. Drivers must be trained to recognize these timeframes in order to make appropriate rest stops for continued safe driving.

- Driver awareness of circadian rhythms. Simply stated, the driver should become aware of his or her own sleep patterns and need for rest. A nap in the daytime may be insufficient to keep the driver awake and alert on the dangerous highway. Regardless, it is best to rest for a fixed period whenever tired. In the event of extreme fatigue, the driver should use discretion and stop driving until it is safe to return to rested driving.

Physical Factors

- Medical conditions. Drivers are required to have annual medical exams to determine fitness for driving because of the strain that extended driving has on the body. When a driver has medical conditions such as diabetes, obesity, or other medical disease and/ or symptoms, it is very important to take appropriately prescribed medications. Some conditions, like epilepsy and diabetes (if uncontrolled), may lead to exhaustion and fatigue or other medical events. Thus, it is extremely important that the driver have regular medical clearance and checkups.
- Emotional issues. Anxiety and depression can influence driving ability. If the driver is taking anxiety medications, like Xanax and Valium, it may have a deleterious effect on the driver's ability to drive safely. When drivers suffer from depression and are prescribed antidepressants, these medications can make the driver sleepy. Alertness is decreased. The driver's perception

and reaction time are reduced. Whenever perception and reaction time are reduced, the driver is a danger on the roads.

- Sleep issues from sleep apnea. Some individuals experience the ill effects of improper rest and sleep due to a disorder called sleep apnea. A person diagnosed with this disorder may attempt to sleep, but during the night, a full level of in REM sleep never occurs due to breathing difficulty. This person wakes up fatigued, without appropriate rest and recovery. A physician can help diagnose sleep apnea through a sleep study. In the event that this condition is confirmed, the individual can be fitted for a CPAP machine, which helps the individual get a restful sleep. Mouth guards are sometimes used in order to help the throat stay open with an appropriate space for breathing air and oxygenating the body. Truck drivers with this condition who go untreated are a hazard on the highways. Motor carriers should routinely check their drivers to see if they have this disorder so that appropriate medical treatment can be given and their fleet of drivers can operate safely without fatigue.

Microsleep is something that occurs when people are extremely tired; it is a very short episode of sleep. It may be only a few seconds. Initially one's eyes start drooping and then they close entirely. Drivers may experience micro sleep if they are indulging in a monotonous task like driving on rural highways with limited periods of barren highway where there are no other obvious drivers, motorists or truck drivers. Microsleep can prove to be extremely dangerous in all tasks, which require ones constant attention, such as driving.

Microsleep is a certain recipe for death. A few seconds of snoozing may end up with an accident that was unintended.

The motorist driving the smaller car is the most likely person to be injured or killed. When truck drivers have micro sleep periods they tend to shift across lanes and can head into oncoming traffic or vehicles adjacent to them. As they awaken they try to overcorrect, which may cause them to drive off of the road or into vehicles to their immediate right or left. Some drivers may go into periods of micro sleep where they drive for a few seconds while asleep and then wake back up. Once the driver starts into a micro sleep, danger lurks. Many drivers do not realize they are in periods of micro sleep. Those drivers continue to drive while fatigued and end up costing the lives of countless others.

Fatigue has been the cause of many major disasters, like the plane crash in 2009 where more than two hundred people were flying from Brazil to France when their route took an unexpected turn and they ended up in the Atlantic Ocean. When the pilot was confronted he said that he only had an hour of sleep at night. In 2013, in the eastern United States, the engineer of a large train fell asleep due to fatigue. The train was going 82 mph right before the crash and was heading into a precarious curve when it should have been slowing to 30 mph. The train jumped the tracks and derailed with several railroad cars pouring into the Harlem River. Four persons were killed and more than sixty were injured. Truck drivers, like train operators and airline pilots, require sufficient rest and sleep so that they do not become fatigued, have episodes of microsleep and momentary lapses of control of the dangerous instruments that they operate. Airlines require pilots not to consume alcohol before operation of the jet. They require them to get sufficient sleep. Motor carriers are no different. They are required by the FMCSR to have drivers who drive rested and sober. Compliance is the problem. While the FAA highly regulates airline pilots, the FMCSA attempts to regulate the truck drivers and motor carriers. The significant difference between the two is that there are many more truck drivers than airline pilots. Compliance monitoring is much more difficult with the number of truck drivers and motor carries simply due to the sheer enormous size of the industry.

9

DISTRACTED DRIVING

D ISTRACTED DRIVING IS a common occurrence for truck drivers, as well as for passenger car drivers. Distracted driving is any activity that diverts a driver's attention away from the primary task of driving. Some forms of distraction are texting, talking on a cell phone, eating and drinking, talking to passengers, reading maps on a telephone or cellular device, using navigation systems that are on the dashboard, and viewing onboard electronic and other devices. These distractions are creating an ever-increasing number of accidents. In 2011, an estimated three hundred eighty seven thousand people were involved in motor vehicle crashes due to distracted driving. In 2012, that number rose to approximate four hundred twenty-one thousand people.

Texting while Driving

Truck drivers text. Many receive dispatch instructions on their cell phones or other electronic satellite devices that randomly pop up, giving them instructions on where to pick up a load. These same devices tell them when the load has to be delivered and give warnings for late delivery. Every time a truck driver looks away from the road, there is an increased chance that an accident will occur.

The average time a person's eyes are off the road while texting is five seconds. When traveling at 55 mph, this five-second period is equivalent to the driver being blindfolded and driving the length of a football field. (2009, VTTI)

The NHTSA acknowledged in 2013 that distracted driving of all kinds, including the use of handheld cell phones, is a growing hazard. The same agency did a study that indicated at least one hundred thousand drivers are texting and more than six hundred thousand drivers are using handheld phones at any given moment of the day while operating a car, truck, or commercial motor vehicle. These statistics are not only staggering, they are understudied. Many trial lawyers know that the amount of accidents caused by drunk drivers is less than the amount caused by drivers who take their eyes off the road long enough to dial a phone number on a cellular device, send a text message, or respond to a text message.

A study conducted by David Swedler at the Johns Hopkins Bloomberg School of Public Health titled, "Epidemiology of Distracted Driving and Research into Distracted Driving among Truck Drivers," concluded that 69 percent of American drivers talk on the phone and 31 percent text while driving. The same study, relying on Olson, et al. (2009) concluded the truck drivers spend up to 60 percent of their driving time on some tertiary activity and 12 percent of their time on some phone-related task. The study also found that motor vehicle-related accidents are the leading cause of occupational fatalities in the United States, causing over two thousand deaths per year. The study period was between 2003 and 2009. They found that commercial drivers suffer 3.7 fatalities per billion vehicle miles traveled, quoting Lyman and Braver (2003). They also found that trucking and trucking courier services have the highest cost of occupational injuries and illnesses in the United States, following the study by Bradley, et al. (2004).

The authors noted a study from Olson, et al., FMCSA report No. 09-042, which evaluated the odds ratios for safety critical events for commercial truck drivers. The ratios were fairly high, showing text messages at a critically high level of 23.24. Writing on a pad or notebook was found to be at the level of 8.98. Looking at a map was at the level of 7.02. Dialing a cell phone was at the level of 5.93. Reaching for electronic devices was at a level of 6.72. Talking on a hands-free cellular device indicated a much lower critical event level of only 0.44.

The same study noted that by 2010, twenty-three states and the District of Columbia had banned texting while driving, while six states and the District of Columbia had banned handheld phone use while driving. This same author noted that in 2009, President Obama prohibited federal employees from texting while driving. In January 2010, the FMCSR banned commercial drivers from texting while driving. FMCSA -2009-0370. In December 2011, the NTSB recommended a nationwide ban on all CWPD for all drivers.

The results of this particular study found that the truck drivers killed in distracted driving crashes amounted to 1,007 deaths during the study period. The fatality rate was 0.321 per billion vehicle miles traveled. For all other vehicle occupants killed in crashes involving distracted driving for truck drivers, the rate was much higher, at 3,942 deaths. This resulted in a fatality rate of 1.101 per billion vehicle miles traveled.

The same author concluded that the 2010 FMCSA rule banning texting while driving for truck drivers was associated with the 41 percent to 47 percent decrease in fatalities to all vehicle occupants and crashes involving distracted truck drivers. Regardless of the FMCSA ban, truck driver-related crashes from distracted driving while texting remains a serious problem for all motorists on US highways.

Any interested person can go to Google or other search engines online and find a rapidly growing number of distracted driving statistics from various governmental and private studies. Many of you have probably seen the billboards across the nation's highways talking about texting while driving and the dangers associated with it. This public information movement will hopefully lead to less text-related accidents.

It is suggested that truck drivers should be required to pull over before looking at texts. An onboard device could be developed and installed in the cab of tractor-trailers and other large commercial vehicles and large trucks that would stop a signal from being received until the truck is in park. A simple device like this could be created and become a mandatory piece of equipment for each and every large truck in the United States. Many injuries and deaths would be prevented. While the costs associated with placement of this device might seem prohibitive to the trucking industry, a cost-benefit analysis would lead to the conclusion that the cost of lost lives outweighs the requirement that all trucking companies install devices to prohibit communication or texting until the vehicle is in park or fully stopped.

Truck drivers realize how heavy and dangerous their tractor-trailers are. They are taught by the trucking industry that the heavier the vehicle is, the more massive it becomes. In turn, the mass and force of the truck becomes more dangerous. Taking five seconds of time from a proper view of the roadway is more than ample time to lead to an accident.

Even so-called hands-free driving requires a momentary distraction from the operator of the vehicle or driver of the truck. That amount of distraction is all it takes to lead to an accident. Safety should be the foremost thought in all drivers' minds. Motor carriers must teach truck drivers not to look at devices that will distract them from the roadway in any manner.

What can be done?

The FMCSA needs to implement stronger safety protocols requiring trucking companies to install devices that prevent driver texting. Lobbyists for the trucking industry do their best with the help of legislators, senators, and congressmen to prevent these laws from being introduced. At some point, logic should outweigh money from lobbyists and trucking companies. Safety systems to protect the nation and motoring public must be implemented. Regulations must be increased and made stricter. Motor carriers must be brought into compliance through increased audits and roadside inspections. Only then will the number of injuries and deaths due to texting and driving be decreased.

In Germany, there are stringent laws that mobile phones cannot be used as long as the engine is running. This is a great step forward. The same types of laws have been implemented in the Netherlands. The United Kingdom has implemented a similar ban, making exceptions for emergency calls. The United Arab Emirates follows such a law very strictly. In one instance, a United Arab Emirates minister was fined for using his mobile phone while driving. The United States must take similar steps to help with public safety. The European nations and several other countries are recognizing the need for making driving while texting illegal. The US Federal government must make a mandatory law that protects drivers in all states and not just a few.

Talking on a Cell Phone While Driving a Truck

Texting on cell phones is just one of the many dangers associated with cellular devices. Talking on a cell phone can also be deadly. The time it takes to dial a number manually can be enough time for a momentary lapse in a view of the road. Looking down at a cell phone to see who is calling takes several seconds. Answering the phone may take a second or two. Every second counts.

Talking on cellular phones diverts the driver's attention from the roadway. Hands-free devices allowing motorists to keep their hands on the steering wheel and eyes on the road are now very common.

A study at Carnegie Mellon University has shown that the use of hands-free cellular devices does not help reduce the risk of accidents. Reports and studies have indicated that just listening to a voice over a speaker, without holding the cellular device, can cause a 37 percent decrease in the activity in the person's parietal lobe section of the brain. The parietal lobe is linked to managing spatial layouts and tasks.

One study from Utah University compared conversations the driver has on the phone with conversations between a driver and passenger. It established that a driver having a conversation on the phone while driving is four times more likely to cause an accident than a driver who is simply talking on the phone to a passenger. Perhaps the reason is that the person on the phone becomes more concentrated on the phone discussion than the person driving and interacting with a passenger.

A study by David L Strayer, et al., titled, "A Comparison of the Cell Phone Driver and the Drunk Driver," was conducted at the University of Utah at Salt Lake City, Utah. This study attempted to determine the relative impairment associated with conversing on a cellular telephone while driving. The purpose of the study was to provide a direct comparison of the driving performance of the driver on a cell phone and a drunk driver. The study was conducted in a controlled laboratory testing setting. For the intoxicated drivers, they used the blood alcohol concentration of 0.08 percent weight/volume. They found that when drivers were conversing on either a hand-held or hands-free cell phone, their braking reactions were delayed and they were involved in more traffic accidents than when they were not conversing on a cell phone. They found that when drivers were intoxicated from ethanol they exhibited a more aggressive driving style, which included following the vehicle immediately in front of them very closely and applying more force when braking. The conclusion was that in the case of the cell phone driver, the impairments appeared to be attributable, in large part, to the diversion of attention from the processing of information necessary for the safe operation of the motor vehicle. They referred to two prior studies as reference for their conclusions. (Strayer, et al., 2003) (Strayer and Johnston, 2001)

What Can Be Done to Decrease Cell Phone Usage?
The State of Alabama has prevented drivers from using cell phones while driving. They are not permitted to use them for texting or making phone calls. Likewise, California has banned all drivers from using their mobile phones, including truck drivers. California is a leader in banning or penalizing drivers from using cell phones while driving.

Several other countries have banned the use of phones while driving, including Brazil, Australia, Argentina, New Zealand, Italy, and the United Kingdom. Some countries, like Japan, have regulated cell phone use to such an extent that they are banning the use of hands-free devices due to the recognition of dangers and hazards associated with the attention-span problems discussed previously. The manufacturers of mobile devices and automobile manufacturers' installation of computerized, hands-free devices or Bluetooth-type devices are now a major selling point for cars. It will be quite some time before the United States issues laws that will reduce profitability of the cellular phone makers or the car manufacturers. Indeed, it may not happen in the next decade.

With the development of the traffic camera that gives tickets out to drivers who are speeding, a similar development for drivers talking on cell phones should be implemented. Substantial fines to drivers who speak on phones could be imposed. For truck drivers who are caught speaking on a cell phone while driving, the truck driver could be given a ticket, which would then be reported directly to the commercial motor carrier that they drive for. This would then be provided to the FMCSA to be logged into the Safer System website. Drivers who get multiple tickets for driving while talking on the phone could then easily be screened from a central system so that motor carriers could avoid those drivers that fail to follow the rules.

Many smaller companies, like utility companies and cable companies, routinely message their drivers on cell phones and other types of devices. It is foreseeable that a person that receives a message to go to a certain jobsite will be attempting to look at that message while driving in order to figure out where their next stop should be. The simple way to eliminate this would be to have the driver call into dispatch every fifteen minutes to determine where the new job will be. Obviously, this would take additional employees and with the development of computerization, many companies have simply gone to message board systems in order to save profit. With the number of accidents rising due to these types of incidents, perhaps profits should be forgiven in order to improve safety and spare lives. Only true action will help to reduce and eliminate dangerous fleet truck drivers on the nation's roadways and highways. These accidents are so commonplace that they provide an abundant supply of motor vehicle accident cases for personal injury attorneys who recognize how dangerous the development of the cellular phone system has been.

10

DRIVING TOO FAST TO MEET DELIVERY DEADLINES

TRUCK DRIVERS FACE enormous job pressures due to the regulatory nature of the occupation, combined with the on-time delivery and maximum hours-of-service rules under the FMCSR, which create a complex environment for the truck driver much different from many professions.

The on-time delivery requirement and meeting the maximum hours-of-service regulations under the FMCSR are likely the most significant causes of truck driver stress. Safe motor carriers do not make their drivers violate the hours-of-service rules. However, smaller companies and motor carriers who do not care about safety push their drivers to meet these on-time deliveries at whatever cost. The drivers know that if they do not arrive on time, they will be punished, reprimanded, or fired. This illogical industry rule causes accidents, death, and carnage. Smaller motor carriers with fewer truck drivers and employees usually violate the hours-of-service rules more than the larger carriers with adequate fleets.

Truck Drivers are Harassed by Dispatch Supervisors to Deliver as Fast as Possible

The motor carrier industry has been set up by the overall industry to get deliveries to a customer as fast as possible, on time, undamaged, and shipped at the lowest possible cost. This industry rule has created a substantial danger and hazard to all motorists on US highways. The reason for this is quite simple. All personnel, from the driver all the way up to the owner of the company, are trying to follow the same rule of mandatory on-time deliveries regardless of the cost of human life. There are only two ways that motor carriers can reach the goal of on-time delivery. The first is to have sufficient drivers, such that they can drive within the maximum hours-of-service rules, and the second is to operate with an insufficient number of truck drivers who are forced to drive over the maximum hours-of-service rules to meet the deadlines. Systems of compensation are developed that dock pay for everyone down the line, including the management, supervisors, dispatch officers, bills of lading personnel, and ultimately the drivers. A truck driver may drop off a load at 6:00 a.m. in one city and be told that he must be clear across the country later that day for another pickup or delivery.

This makes for weary and fatigued truck drivers who are in fear of losing of their jobs. Truck drivers get reprimanded when they make late deliveries. If they get too many reprimands, they lose their job. There are a number of reasons why this hazardous system is in place, which are discussed below.

The Customer Mindset has Changed Over the Last Several Decades to a Need-Based System Designed Around Timely Delivery

Years ago, businesses would stock inventory, keeping a fairly decent supply on hand. Over the last several decades, as production and inventory costs have risen, many businesses have just showrooms and no actual inventory. A customer may come into a furniture store hoping to buy a living room set to take home the same day. Unfortunately, the business does not stock that inventory. It is only on display for sale by order. The customer wants to get their new furniture urgently. The store promises that they can have the purchased furniture in a certain period of time. The furniture is not yet built, but will be built once the order is placed. The minute the order is placed, the shipment process begins. This order will have to be delivered within a certain period of time to a certain place. Customers sometimes cancel shipments after orders do not get delivered on time. Society's need for instant gratification, combined with the inability of sellers of goods to keep sufficient stock on hand for immediate sale, has changed how shipments works in a modern era.

Worldwide manufacturing and distribution from China to Argentina is changing the economic marketplace, such that the competition worldwide has now lowered the production prices of many goods sold in the common marketplace. An example would be the prices of television sets, which continue to drop in price, year by year, as the television sets get more sophisticated. A plasma television set that cost $15,000 ten years ago now sells for $1500. Best Buy and other retailers research and plan to buy at the lowest possible wholesale price for the goods. Once sufficient orders are anticipated or completed, they begin the shipment process and compel rapid delivery systems to be in place in order to satisfy customer appetite.

Once the order is placed, the shipper is contacted to set up an anticipated pickup and delivery time. The trucking company assigns a truck driver to pick up a shipment and deliver it to a certain destination by a specified time and date. The faster the process is meant to be, the faster the shipment deadline becomes. Once the speed of delivery becomes an issue, safety is cast aside or is minimized. The reason safety is cast aside is because it costs money and time to create, plan, implement, and follow down the motor carrier chain of distribution a safe plan for shipment. When time gets in the way, safety goes out the door.

Time of delivery has become so important that retailers like Amazon are now testing miniature drones to deliver to customers from shipping distribution centers across the country and seeking FAA approval in order to have thousands of miniature drones deliver products dropped straight to a door of a customer. It is anticipated that with the increasing needs of consumers, combined with worldwide competition, that shipping needs will become faster than they are in now in 2014. As stated, the faster the product must be delivered, the least likely safety will be involved in the delivery process.

Companies like Amazon, Best Buy, and others understand that the speed of delivery, combined with the lowest cost of delivery, will bring the most profit. As delivery needs grow, trucking and shipment needs grow, thereby creating an over-all rapid on-time delivery process to please the customer and to increase profit. Profit is obviously higher when shipment costs are faster and lower.

Consumer expectation has risen rapidly and unrealistically. The faster a company delivers its products and services to the customer, the more orders it ends up getting. Ultimately, the higher a company's net revenue and profit is, the faster the entire shipment industry must move.

Competition is Increasing Which Makes Shipments More Unsafe

With worldwide competition increasing, trucking companies and their drivers must move faster and faster in order to please consumers. The weaker and smaller companies in the motor carrier industry collapse due to their inability to compete with the larger motor carriers. Larger trucking companies can deliver goods faster and cheaper. Those motor carriers and truck drivers who log behind will likely disappear from the marketplace and file bankruptcy. Motor carriers develop shipment models and use software that has built-in time deadlines that provide notices to dispatch operators that a shipment is too far away to meet the time deadline. When a shipment appears to be running late, the notification process causes the dispatch officer to notify the truck driver that he or she is behind schedule. The truck driver then has two choices: speed to try to make up for lost time or drive longer and over the maximum hours-of-service limits to make the shipment arrive on time. This is how the entire shipment process breaks down and becomes foreseeably hazardous.

A trucking company that cannot provide the same services their larger competitors do will lose business to those larger companies, due mostly to late deliveries. Trucking companies know that they will go out of business if they don't meet the time demands of the purchasing customers. Everyone is in a hurry and very few care about safety.

This results in motor carriers and dispatch officers pushing and forcing their truck drivers to drive at top speeds to deliver the packages in an unrealistic time deadline that cannot possibly be met without violating the FMCSR maximum hours-of-service rules. Non-compliance with maximum hours-of-service rules and other regulations under the FMCSR cause serious death and injury to thousands of people across the United States each year.

Some larger trucking companies try to avoid violating the system by hiring a sufficient numbers of truck drivers, as well as relief drivers. When drivers are known to be out of time to drive, dispatch can send in a relief driver who will pick up the load from its present location and give the truck driver time for rest. The shipment continues attached to a new tractor with a driver who is rested. Unfortunately, the number of motor carriers that try to be safe are few and far between.

The Threat of Becoming Unemployed

All truck drivers are aware of the threat of becoming unemployed because of their failure to deliver on time. Truck drivers are usually paid on a per-mile basis. When a trucking company pays a truck driver on a per-mile basis or on a per-pound basis, the truck driver becomes aware that driving more miles in a shorter period of time leads to greater gross and net profit and revenue for that truck driver. Many truck drivers are independent contractors who lease themselves out to larger motor carriers. The truck drivers know that they are going to have to comply with whatever dispatch requires and that if they don't deliver on time, they will be fired or reprimanded.

Many trucking companies reduce the rate of pay per mile for truck drivers when they are late on their delivery times. These punishment systems cause the truck driver to lose income. Truck drivers, like everyone else in the world, have to be concerned with meeting monthly obligations for rent or mortgage payments, car payments, utilities, food, and all other obligations of daily life. The fact that they must routinely violate the FMCSR maximum hours-of-service rules is not something that is taught in truck driving schools. This is a learned behavior from the motor carriers and dispatch officers that supervise the delivery routes for the goods.

Once the driver starts driving in the real world setting, the driver learns that there are two different rules that are followed. The industry overtly professes to hold itself up to a higher standard, stating that it does not push truck drivers to violate the maximum hours-of-service rule. The real standard followed is one of rapid, on-time delivery and overworked truck drivers. Lawyers who litigate against the trucking industry know how false the industry standard of safety really is. The Safer System website snapshot allows any person to view thousands of motor carriers and check their safety record. A random check of any group of motor carriers will find that it is commonplace to find safety statistics showing drivers who should have been taken out of service for a myriad of reasons. Much of the time, those reasons are for unsafe driving without enough remaining time on their logs and/

or overloading tractor-trailers to drive a heavier load farther across the country to be paid more gross and net profit. These truck drivers and motor carriers do not follow the safety rules set forth under the FMCSR. Indeed, just the opposite is true. Safety records of motor carriers on the Safer System website establish that many companies violate the rules on a daily and weekly basis without punishment. The motor carriers are aware that the funding limitations of the FMCSA and DOT, combined with the funding limitations of state and local governments and their policing officers and agencies, makes it impossible to completely police and enforce compliance with the FMCSR.

Many truck drivers purchase their tractor unit or larger trucks through financing, which means they may have monthly payments that are sometimes higher than a mortgage payment. The payments must be made or the truck driver will lose the truck. In order to meet the payments, the truck driver has to drive a certain set amount of miles to meet the minimum amount of miles on a per-mile pay system to obtain enough pay for the tractor payment, insurance and taxes, and fuel for the vehicle. This well-known fact causes truck drivers to knowingly drive too fast and over hours to meet deadlines.

The global economic crisis has affected the shipping industry, just as it has affected business worldwide. Back in 2008, when the recession was getting underway, shipping started to drop as the economy slowed and the recession progressed. As the economy slowly turned around since 2009 and beyond, the shipping needs of manufacturers started to increase steadily. With the shipping needs of goods globally increasing on an annual basis, an accompanying need for more shipping follows. As the shipments increase, there is a corresponding increase in unsafe driving statistics, which are measured by the DOT.

The truck driver's fear of unemployment is a major driving force in his or her life. Truck drivers are in the middle class of society. Independent drivers can make a living, but they never really get ahead due to the high costs of operation of a tractor-trailer across the United States. These drivers do not intend to be unsafe drivers, they simply are trying to meet their financial obligations and raise their families like everyone else. Unfortunately, motor carriers and the shipping deadlines do not allow them to safely comply with their job duties. Pushing the driver to exceed human tolerance limits causes accidents.

Motor carriers who reduce the pay by mile to the truck driver and those that reduce their pay for not meeting an on-time delivery are causing grief and tragedy on highways by pushing their drivers to an unrealistic level, just to make an increased profit. The government can step in and mandate the use of onboard computer systems and satellite tracking that will send signals to the motor carriers when a truck driver is approaching maximum hours-of-service violations and will run out of time. Indeed, a system can be set in place where the computerized onboard system would give preliminary notice simultaneously to the truck driver and the motor carrier that the driver is out of time. If the driver did not stop working at the appropriate maximum hour limit, then the ignition could be automatically turned off, similar to an intoxilyzer unit for a drunk driver. The drunk driver must blow into the unit every fifteen minutes or the car will cease to operate. The truck could be programmed to give the truck driver a one-, two-, or three-hour notice that he is running out of time. As the truck approached the last hour of driving, it could flash a warning with a countdown to the truck driver that he only has so many remaining minutes to find a truck stop or motel to pull over and rest. At the appropriate expiration of time, the tractor ignition would simply cease working for a period of hours until the truck driver could start the vehicle back up and drive after sufficient rest. This would cause the motor carrier and dispatch officers to send in a relief driver with a new tractor.

The industry does not want to have safety systems in place like this because it would cause a loss of profits to the overall trucking industry nationwide.

The High Level of Compliance Violations is not Recognized

The general public does not understand how serious the level of noncompliance is. Trucking companies go to great lengths to advertise public service announcements about the dangers of tractor-trailers, trying to blame drivers for failing to recognize the dangers associated with being near a truck or tractor-trailer. These public service announcements fail to mention the fact that the trucking industry in general is causing millions of injuries and deaths because of its failure to comply with the FMCSR mandatory regulations.

Trucking schools that do recognize the dangers associated with failure to comply with the FMCSR fail to train the drivers on how important it is to strictly follow the regulations. These schools don't teach real-world practices. It is clear the truck drivers are not taught in truck driving school that they will be required to follow dispatch commands about pickups and deliveries, or that they will be reprimanded, receive pay cuts, and be terminated if they do not fall in line with the demands of the dispatch officers. If this training were put into place at truck driving schools and during orientation at a new job with a motor carrier, accident rates would fall. If a system was actually implemented that would turn off the ignition system once drivers were out of hours, compliance with the FMCSR could be readily achieved and accident rates would fall.

Trucking schools do not teach the drivers about the dangers of fatigue and excessive tiredness. Schools should teach the drivers that they should immediately report their trucking companies to the FMCSA when they make them drive over their maximum hours-of-service. The problem with this logic is that once the truck driver is out on the road and trying to meet the demands of their financial obligations, they become a pawn in the motor carrier distribution system. This is not to say that all truck drivers are in noncompliance. All it takes is one truck driver to violate the rules for an accident to take place. When you take one truck driver who fails to comply and multiply that driver by one thousand more unsafe drivers, the gravity of the situation becomes clear.

Approximately five hundred thousand truck-related accidents occur in the United States on an annual basis. It is clear that the entire industry needs to change to become more regulated with a mandated higher level of compliance. Financial incentives, such as tax relief, should be introduced as legislation in order to give motor carriers that have safer driving statistics a reduction on taxes. Motor carriers who place onboard computer systems with satellite devices into their tractor-trailers so that they can monitor the hours-of-service limits of their drivers should also be given tax credits and additional tax reduction benefits for purchasing these costly devices.

A regulatory system needs to be implemented where truck drivers with a certain maximum number of violations must be retrained in trucking school and then followed more closely. A certain motor carrier in the state of Missouri actually proposed to the DOT that each of their drivers should be able to have sixty safety violations in any given six-month period of time before being reprimanded. This logic was based on the argument that the industry has trouble hiring enough drivers due to a known problem with driver turnover that reaches as high as 150 percent turnover rate per year.

That company had a temporary loss of their DOT license, which required an appeal to a federal circuit court. Even though their DOT license was reinstated, it did not change the manner of their compliance with the safety regulations.

Truck drivers who work for companies like this particular one know that the company has a low safety score and choose to work for that company knowing that they will push them to the end limits of human capability. Those truck drivers are complicit in their choice to work for that company and other companies following similar unsafe driving practices, because they know that the company will not likely terminate or reprimand them, no matter how high their safety violation rate becomes. Those drivers know that they can drive one hundred or more hours a week and violate the FMCSR maximum hours-of-service rules without fear of retribution or punishment from the motor carrier. Many motor carriers exist that are similar to the company being discussed.

When truck drivers and motor carriers implied or expressly agree to violate the FMCSR in order to make money, those drivers and their supervisors and owners of the companies should be stopped from harming innocent drivers on US roads.

Other Types of Job Pressures Causing Stress on Truck Drivers Leading to Accidents

Most of the time, employers only take into account the distance the truck driver has to travel to complete a job. They do not consider the several other factors that are involved in completing a job out on the road. Some of the different factors that may cause a truck driver to become late on their schedule are:

- Heavy traffic due to normal traffic and/or roadside emergencies
- Equipment breakdowns that are foreseeable, like traveling with worn-out tires and brakes
- Traffic jams due to other accidents in areas where bad roads are known to exist or where construction is known to exist
- Traveling in rain, snowstorms, high winds, and other bad weather conditions where the truck driver should drive slower or cease operation entirely and wait for the weather to clear

- Equipment malfunctioning unexpectedly due to avoidance of warning lights on engine temperature and low oil or antifreeze
- Delivery instructions which have an incorrect address
- Failure to provide satellite direction systems to guide the driver to the place of delivery using the shortest route possible

How Does the Present Regulatory System Punish the Speeding Truck Driver?

The regulations in the FMCSR discussed above make it clear that drivers of large trucks are prevented from and should not speed. There are serious consequences for a truck driver who repeatedly speeds. Some of the consequences can include:

- The driver can lose their DOT CDL commercial driver's license
- The driver can cause an accident resulting in death and be punished for reckless or negligent homicide
- The driver can cause huge monetary losses to a driver of a car or passenger in the car when he/she speeds and causes an accident with a serious and life-altering injury
- The driver can be suspended and lose pay
- The driver can be in a Rule of Three disciplinary system where the third speeding citation results in the loss of their job
- The driver can be reported to computerized hiring information services like DAC Services so that the driver is not hired by other motor carriers
- The driver can be subject to civil and criminal penalties, including jail time
- The driver can have a permanent revocation of their CDL driver's license
- The driver can be killed as a result of speeding

It is estimated that approximately thirteen thousand lives are lost each year due to speeding alone. This number is only increasing year by year. About five thousand of these deaths are caused by speeding trucks. Mandatory regulations requiring governors and satellite onboard monitoring systems could eliminate many deaths related to speeding.

In addition to the issuance of mandatory regulations requiring the use of governors and satellite onboard monitoring systems, or the use of cameras at known, dangerous high-traffic locations that utilize onboard computerized systems to slow the trucks, there are other types of safety-related methods that can be utilized to stop a truck driver from speeding. Obviously, the mandatory regulations, governors, and satellite onboard systems are the best prevention methods possible. The reason that they are not presently mandated is because the trucking industry does not want to spend the necessary monies on the purchase of the devices. The trucking industry utilizes a lobbying effort that spends hundreds of millions of dollars with Congress and state legislatures to stop and prevent the mandatory regulation of the industry. The industry makes a fortune and can afford to line the pockets of state and federal senators and congressman to accept bribes and kickbacks. The old-boy system has always existed and always will. Unfortunately, Congress can be bought by unscrupulous lobbyists working for the trucking industry.

The following steps can be taken to stop truck drivers from speeding on the roads:

- The trucking company can provide weekly safety meetings to outline the importance of safe driving, which includes not speeding, and can provide comprehensive testing after each safety meeting
- The trucking company can utilize training and orientation systems like the Smith System and the J.J. Keller

system of driver training, which reinforces the dangers of speeding to the driver

- The trucking company can impose a disciplinary system with the Rule of Three and let the drivers know that after three strikes, they are out of a job
- The trucking company can retrain the driver after any accident about how not to speed
- The trucking company can do annual motor vehicle record checks on the driver's violation history and then reprimand and/or fire the unsafe drivers
- The trucking company can set up a reward system to compensate good drivers and punish the drivers who fail to comply with safety systems
- The trucking company can provide annual reviews that alter the pay rate for good and bad drivers
- The trucking company can have dispatch monitor the distance between two points, which allows for the tracking of the driver's speed since a known speed will generally reach a known destination in a mean or average time that can be calculated out with systems available to the dispatchers
- The trucking company can stop requiring on-time deliveries
- The trucking company can allow the drivers to be paid when they are over their legal hours while they stop to rest

Policies of Trucking Companies

The deliver-on-time model of transportation is a policy of each individual trucking company or motor carrier. The safer companies only dispatch when they know a driver has enough time to make the delivery safely. Computer algorithm programs can assist by calculating a driver's daily and weekly hours left available under the FMCSR. Some companies use Qualcomm and other software and satellite systems to track the delivery schedule and calculate the time available. The main reason many smaller motor carriers avoid using these policies and products is due to the costs required to purchase and continue to use them. They prioritize profits over lives. They do so knowingly and make a conscious decision not to pay for the safer tracking system. When this happens, it is the motor carrier that is causing the driver to drive fatigued and violate the hours-of-service rules.

A simple principle of education can be used to help provide a safe driver. Teach, test, test again, and then teach at regular intervals with testing to see if the driver and student has learned what is being taught. The Smith System is a defensive driving manual for motor carriers. J.J. Keller writes manuals for teaching and produces videotape classroom training for each and every specific item of safety training that is necessary. The good truck driver is taught to anticipate and perceive hazards before they arise and concurrently with their rapid appearance on a road.

Motor carriers design compensation systems like being paid by the mile. This, in turn, means that the more a truck driver drives per day, the more compensation he is paid. This is one of the most dangerous systems created for driver and motor carrier safety. This type of system is the antithesis of the safety-minded programs. Pay by the mile leads to driving over hours and maintaining of two sets of logbooks, one to show real time and the other to show fake time in compliance with the FMCSR.

Another profit-driven system is the "on-time" delivery requirement. Years ago, Domino's Pizza was sued for the promise of pizza delivery in thirty minutes or it would be free. Their drivers rushed to deliver pizza. The obvious occurred. Rapid delivery led to accidents and unsafe conditions. This same system in motor carriers leads to accidents, crashes, severe injuries, and deaths. All motor carriers should implement systems of safety that allow the driver a grace period on delivery when they have short hours remaining on their hours per day and week.

Paper Logbooks Are Falsified

Falsification of logs by truck drivers is a leading cause of motor vehicle accidents. Lawyers who represent truck drivers in worker's compensation cases are able to ask their truck driver clients for an honest answer as to whether they actually use two sets of books. One would be surprised to find out how many truck drivers will admit that they routinely drive one hundred to one hundred twenty hours per week and use two sets of books. One set is for their true miles and the other set is for the police, law enforcement, and highway patrol officers who stop them in roadside audits.

It takes a great amount of fraud for the truck driver to keep the two sets of books. A motor carrier can eliminate this by using an onboard computer system and/or satellite tracking system that records the location of the tractor-trailer at any given moment in time. Software systems are then able to determine that the truck driver is over the allowable hours. This type of safety system is not always used because it proves that the truck drivers are over hours. When an accident occurs, the satellite system can often lead to a huge damage verdict against the motor carrier. Some motor carriers look at the satellite systems as a means of causing them increased damages in the event of accidents by their drivers, so they intentionally choose not to use them.

Drivers are inventive and can think of hundreds of ways to falsify logs. Drivers can simply write down the wrong time for each event on a log, or write that they are off duty when they are on duty. They can write that they are sleeping when they are not sleeping and are actually driving. When they are doing actual work, such as loading and unloading at a shipment point, they can record this as off-duty time when it is legally required to be reported as on-duty time. Clever drivers can think of many ways to defraud the law enforcement professionals and the FMCSA. Unfortunately, many of these logbooks are never found until the drivers have an accident after being on the road for too long.

Most truck drivers are asked to record:

- The time that they spend on duty doing their job
- The time they spend off duty after doing their job
- The time they spend sleeping while off the job
- The time they spend driving out on the road
- The time they spend performing work activities like loading and unloading, which is required on-duty time
- The time they spend taking rest periods and days off duty

Truck drivers are required to send in their logs at the end of every seven days in order to receive their pay. The written logs are typically in duplicate or triplicate so that the truck driver keeps a copy. In post-accident depositions of truck drivers, it is surprising to find how many drivers do not keep a copy of their actual logs. The trucking companies take the original logs and scan them into software systems. Most of the software systems are automatically programmed to destroy them six months after the date of the accident. Since the originals are destroyed, the lawyers who try to find the actual logs and wait more than six months to file suit or fail to send out spoliation letters to preserve evidence quickly learn that they have lost the most critical evidence for a case. The original logs are the real logs. They prove what really happened.

Many trucking experts will take the actual logs and then track them with bills of lading, fuel receipts and invoices, turnpike toll receipts, weighing station receipts, and other documents that are maintained by the driver and motor carrier, to actually reconstruct the roads and miles driven. It is quite surprising to find how many times the different documents do not correlate with one another. When the correlation between documents does not appear accurate, then the lawyer knows that the driver was falsifying logs and lying about their true miles and hours. Many severe truck accidents are caused by truck drivers that lie about their miles driven and their hours of service.

Truck drivers who are paid by the mile or by the weight have more incentive to falsify logs. The further they drive, the more money they make. The heavier the load, the more money they make. These incentives to truck drivers by motor carriers are intentionally created to move more shipments and product across the roads at a cheaper cost to the motor carrier and shipper. The truck driver is simply the means to the end.

Legislators continue to introduce legislation that mandates that paper logs be discontinued. The discontinuance of paper logs is something that should be mandated for each and every truck driver in the United States. Regardless of the cost of electronic onboard recorders, also known as EOBRs, their use should be mandatory, with no exception.

Electronic Logbooks
Truck drivers have been using paper logs since as early as the 1930s. They have always been required to document their starting time, rest periods, and sleep time, as well as their off-duty time. In the 1990s, a new technology was developed to eliminate paper logs. One of the companies that developed these electronic logbooks is called Werner Enterprises. The company developed a paperless logbook, which worked with the help of a GPS system. Werner Enterprises worked in conjunction with the DOT to develop these electronic paperless logs, which would eliminate driver falsification of logs. Since that time, many other companies have developed similar systems. Qualcomm is one of the well-known companies that

many major trucking companies use. Companies that use Qualcomm and similar satellite tracking systems that allow them to know the exact place and location of each and every driver and tractor are companies that are at least trying to utilize a safer system to protect the motoring public.

These electronic and satellite systems help to eliminate driver ability to falsify logs. These same systems allow the motor carrier to provide safer drivers who are not driving over maximum time restrictions. The margin of human error is minimized. The ability of the truck driver to intentionally and fraudulently falsify their logs is minimized. Truck drivers still can figure ways to get around electronic logs. The inventiveness of humankind can never be underestimated. There is and always will be a need for better and safer tracking systems.

The creation and the invention of electronic logbooks with satellite systems as a replacement of paper logbooks is a much safer methodology for tracking drivers' hours of service. It helps protect lives. Electronic logbooks help eliminate driver fatigue. As advancements in technology continue to grow, electronic logbooks will continue to grow in use in the motor carrier industry.

Truckload Carriers Association found at www.truckload. org and FleetOwner found at FleetOwner.com evaluated different types of electronic logbook software in a webinar in August of 2014. The presentation advocated the use of electronic logbooks because they are durable, convenient, and help prevent falsification.

This type of electronic logbook recording offers the following benefits to motor carriers:

- They promote greater fuel efficiency for the entire fleet of trucks
- Safety and compliance issues can be management in a much easier fashion

- Electronic logbooks promote compliance with the FMCSR maximum hours-of-service regulations
- Fleet productivity is improved
- Net operating revenues are improved
- CSA compliance with the seven basic rules of CSA is made easier
- Trip reports and fuel reports are managed in a much easier fashion
- Motor carriers can look for and evaluate red-flag critical events much easier
- The software allows real-time evaluation of critical factors in everyday fleet management
- Logbooks are managed and maintained in a much more usable format
- Beginner drivers can be monitored for errors in order to better train the drivers
- Helps with logbook violations and tracks bad drivers

These systems help to reduce hours-of-service violations at an amazing rate of approximately a 63 percent reduction in violations, while simultaneously reducing the driver out-of-service rates by 74 percent. On-time delivery becomes easier. Customers are happier and profits increase.

11

INSURANCE REQUIREMENTS FOR COMMERCIAL MOTOR VEHICLES

T HE TRUCKING INDUSTRY was created for the transportation of cargo across interstate and intrastate roads and highways. The trucking industry has always looked for ways to avoid the payment of compensation to injured motorists who are sometimes catastrophically injured due to the negligence of these large and forceful machines. Laws were created to protect the public for specific legislative reasons. This included the creation of the Motor Carrier Act of 1935, the Motor Carrier Act of 1980, the Bus Regulation Act of 1982, and most recently, the Moving Ahead for Progress in the Twenty-first Century Act. All of these laws were created to protect the motoring public from the negligence of truck drivers and motor carriers.

The DOT has the FMCSA to assist in the promulgation of regulations to promote safety. The FMCSA and DOT helped create and implement the FMCSR, which were written to promote the purpose of the federal regulations. That purpose is to help reduce or prevent truck and bus accidents, injuries, and fatalities.

Part 383.1 of the FMCSR specifically states that the purpose of the FMCSR is to help reduce or prevent truck and bus accidents, injuries, and fatalities by requiring drivers to have a single commercial motor vehicle driver's license and by disqualifying drivers who operate commercial motor vehicles in an unsafe manner.

The purpose of the Interstate Commerce Commission (ICC) statutory law and regulations under the FMCSA is to ensure that a financially responsible party will be available to compensate third persons injured in a collision with an ICC carrier. The regulations were implemented, at least in part, for the purpose of improving highway safety.

These federal laws can only be enforced if insurance is required. When a person has been injured in a commercial motor vehicle accident or tractor-trailer accident, the victim has only one source for compensation—the trucking company and its driver, which leads to the evaluation of insurance for the driver and the company they work for. When reviewing the applicable insurance requirements, a lawyer will normally seek the information about the driver, the motor carrier that the driver is working for, and any companies that are leasing the driver and tractor. Many independent truck drivers would not carry insurance unless it was required. Many of the smaller trucking companies and independent drivers are not financially stable. The accidents that they cause lead to immense human suffering. In many states, the laws allow for naming the insurance company that insures the driver and tractor as a party defendant to the case. Both federal and state laws have requirements for truck drivers operating on interstate and intrastate highways.

Insurance requirements can be a complicated topic to discuss due to the discrepancies in law. This particular discussion only addresses the federal requirements of insurance as they apply to truck drivers and motor carriers. To thoroughly understand why insurance is required and why the limit needs to be increased, we must look at the past.

During the first half of the twentieth century, interstate motor carriers attempted to protect themselves from liability for negligent drivers by leasing trucks and nominally classifying the drivers who operated the trucks as independent contractors. In order to protect the public from the tortious conduct of the often judgment-proof truck-lessor operators, Congress, in 1956, amended the Interstate Commerce Carrier Act to require interstate motor carriers to assume full direction and control of the vehicles that they leased as if they were the owners of such vehicles. The purpose of the amendment was to ensure that interstate motor carriers would be fully responsible for the maintenance and operation of the leased equipment and the supervision of the borrowed drivers, thereby protecting the public from accidents, preventing public confusion about who was financially responsible if accidents occurred, and providing financially responsible defendants.

Federal Commercial Truck Insurance Requirements
The FMCSR, under part 387, requires minimum levels of financial responsibility for motor carriers. Part 387.1 describes the actual purpose of this particular section of the FMCSR and states that the minimum levels of financial responsibility required to be maintained by motor carriers and the purpose of the regulations is to create additional incentives to motor carriers to maintain and operate their vehicles in a safe manner and to ensure that motor carriers maintain an appropriate level of financial responsibility for motor vehicles operated on public highways. Part 387.405 prescribes the limits of liability and mandates that the minimum amounts for cargo or public liability are identical to those prescribed for the motor carriers under 49 CFR 387.303.

Part 387.303 is the federal regulation that provides security for the protracted protection of the public with minimum limits of insurance. There is a difference in how this insurance is interpreted. Typically, one would look at whether or not a vehicle weighs ten thousand pounds or more. Small freight vehicles are those commercial motor vehicles that weigh less than ten thousand pounds. Once a vehicle reaches the level of 10,001 pounds and above, the minimum insurance coverage becomes higher on a mandatory basis.

These weight parameters are significant and determine the motor carrier's mandatory amount of insurance. A vehicle carrying ten thousand pounds is roughly equivalent to five tons. As noted above, the guidelines for trucks that weigh more than ten thousand pounds are usually broken down into two separate categories. Those two categories are separated by type of cargo: normal or hazardous.

Bodily injury liability is specifically defined to mean injury to the body, sickness, or disease, including death resulting from any of these factors. For the purpose of this discussion, this would mean a person, driver, motorcyclist, pedestrian, or other victim of a trucking accident has been in an accident with a truck driver and where the truck driver and/or motor carrier caused bodily harm to that individual. When a lawyer assists a victim who has been injured in a motor vehicle accident with a large truck or big rig, lawyers typically will look at the costs related to past and future medical expenses, past and future wages, economic losses, disability, and other factors related to a bodily injury. Many of these accidents result in substantial injuries that will require surgery, amputation, prosthetics, and long-term medical care. The costs associated with an accident with a large truck can be catastrophic and life-altering costs that the average human being cannot afford. In many instances, the lawyer for an injured victim will have to hire medical experts and life-care experts in order to project the future and lifetime costs associated with the injury.

The term *property damage liability* is defined under part 387.5 to mean damage to or loss of the use of tangible property. In the property damage sense, lawyers are typically looking for the valuation of the damage to cars and other motor vehicles. When a truck drives into a tangible structure or a sign and causes damage to real property, the lawyer will look to obtain compensation for the damage to this property.

Many trucks and motor carriers carry commercial truck cargo coverage. This is a specific type of insurance for cargo that is damaged or destroyed on a particular load. Many times, the insurance will cover full costs of replacement of the damaged cargo. The insurance will pay for and cover the cost of cleanup and other site-specific damage. These large vehicles will oftentimes cause damage to the asphalt and the traveled roadway, which causes a need for repair to the surface of the highway. One accident can cause a million dollars of damage to repair.

The specific types of minimum coverage are generally described in part 387 of the FMCSR. The present categories are set forth below.

Federal Commercial Truck Insurance Minimum Coverage Amounts

Vehicles 10,000 GVW (Gross vehicle weight) or over carrying Nonhazardous Material

- Bodily injury liability $750,000
- Property damage liability $750,000
- Truck cargo coverage $300,000

Vehicles 10,000 GVW (Gross vehicle weight) or over carrying Hazardous Material

- Bodily injury liability $1,000,000
- Property damage liability $1,000,000
- Truck cargo coverage $5,000,000

The transportation of hazardous materials creates a significantly higher minimum amount of coverage due to the catastrophic nature of a potential accident. The harm that can be caused is much greater when the truck driver and motor carrier are transporting dangerous chemicals and materials.

Insurance carriers will evaluate the safety record of the motor carrier in order to determine how high of a premium to charge. Most insurance companies will perform an insurance audit on a yearly basis, where they study the safety factors and FMCSR compliance of the trucking company and motor carrier. If a trucking company has a good safety record, the insurance rates will usually be lower. Some of the worst motor carriers and trucking companies are unable to get liability insurance without having a retained self-insurance level. This means that the insurance company may come in and pay to assist in the event of an accident with the understanding that the motor carrier will pay the first $250,000 or the first $500,000 out of their self-insured retention. Many trucking companies use a self-insured retention in order to avoid some of the higher costs of liability insurance. What these trucking companies fail to understand is that if they had a better safety record, they would be able to get full insurance coverage due to the statistical probability that there would be less chance of an accident by having a higher level of safety.

Your Personal Auto Insurance May Apply to Many Property and Bodily Injury Occurrences.
Insurance requirements for personal auto and motorcycle coverage vary with different mandatory minimum amounts of coverage state by state. Some states provide for what is called no-fault coverage where your own car insurance will pay the first several thousand dollars of your medical bills, as well as your immediate wage loss benefits. Unfortunately, not all states have no-fault laws. This no-fault insurance coverage is also

called Personal Injury Protection benefits or PIP. In order to understand what your state requires for specific types of coverage that are mandatory, you can contact a local attorney or your state insurance commissioner. Many different types of coverage can be purchased.

No-fault, Personal Injury Protection, and Medical Payment Coverage

Many states have insurance laws that require the insurance company to provide a minimum level of no-fault, personal injury protection benefits, or medical payment coverage. These PIP benefits or no-fault laws have no bearing on whether or not the truck driver or motor carrier is at fault. These benefits are simply a quick and efficient means to get immediate compensation for the injuries and wage loss that results from a motor vehicle accident with a large truck.

The issue of fault is completely separate and distinct from whether PIP or medical payment coverage applies. Many people believe that if their insurance company makes a payment, it means that the trucking company was not at fault. The payment by your insurance carrier has absolutely no bearing on whether or not the truck driver or company that he or she drove for was at fault.

Many states allow the driver of a motor vehicle or motorcycle to buy minimum levels of coverage. They also allow a person and their insurance agent to purchase higher levels of coverage if desired.

Caveat emptor or buyer beware best describes the decision-making process when purchasing insurance coverage. If you do not have a good insurance agent who goes out of the way to advise you about the benefits of having higher levels of coverage, then you may be in a position where you have insufficient insurance coverage for the short-term recovery. Insurance agents have a loyalty and duty that is owed to the customer. However, that same insurance agent is usually under what is called a loss-ratio rule with the particular insurance company they sell for. Independent agents will sell policies through many different companies. Regardless, almost all companies place the agent under a specific loss-ratio analysis. When an agent sells an average of one hundred policies of insurance, the underwriting insurance carrier will require analysis of the agent to determine what percentage of every one hundred policies results in a loss. This means that if they sell too many policies to bad drivers who statistically end up with a claim for benefits, the agent may lose his or her license to sell insurance policies to that company. As a result of these insurance industry protocols, it is absolutely necessary that you inquire of your own agent about how much coverage you should purchase.

Uninsured Truck Drivers

The concept of an uninsured truck driver is rare. It does happen. Many independent truck drivers may believe that their policy is in effect when they have, in fact, missed a payment deadline. The policy then lapses and the truck driver becomes uninsured. There are many smaller, independent-contractor trucking companies in larger metropolitan areas who, for whatever reason, fail to purchase insurance on a timely basis. Some of the worst truck drivers actually fail to carry any insurance. They do so intentionally because of the high cost of insurance. In order to protect yourself in the event you are hit by an uninsured truck driver, you can purchase your own policy of insurance.

Almost all fifty states have laws that allow for the purchase of uninsured and underinsured motorist coverage. These are two distinct topics that will be discussed separately. The uninsured motorist coverage is usually equivalent to the state minimum levels of liability coverage. In other words, if you are required to carry $25,000 of coverage and you are hurt, you may have $25,000 of uninsured motorist coverage. Many states will allow you to reject certain limits of uninsured motorist coverage. Some states let you reject the coverage in its entirety. The important thing to remember is that you have to have enough insurance to cover your injuries. While many trucking companies carry $750,000 of coverage or $1 million of coverage, the trucking companies that have a lapse will have zero coverage.

Most individuals do not realize that purchasing liability coverage, as well as uninsured and underinsured motorist coverage, is relatively cheap. You can ask your agent for a quote. In many circumstances, you can purchase $1 million of uninsured motorist and underinsured motorist coverage for a rather small annual fee. You should always carry a minimum of $250,000 of liability coverage per person, with accompanying uninsured and underinsured motorist coverage of the same amount. When you can afford the higher premiums required for additional coverage, it would be wise to carry a minimum amount of $1 million per person. Surprisingly, this may only cost a few hundred dollars extra per year.

In the event that you are hit by an uninsured truck operator or driver, you would make a claim for benefits to your own insurance company for uninsured motorist benefits. The simple fact that you buy $100,000 or $500,000 of insurance coverage does not mean that you have a claim for that value. You have to evaluate the fair amount of your damages as they relate to past and future medical expenses, past and future economic and wage loss, past and future loss of consortium for your spouse who performs household services and other services like replacement services for things you can no longer do. Damages would also include noneconomic losses, such as pain and suffering, disability, loss of enjoyment of life, mental anguish, or loss of time.

The cost of medical treatment continues to escalate. In the present day it is extremely high. Many people do not have health insurance coverage even though federal law now requires everyone to have it. Many simply cannot afford the cost of health insurance because of the high monthly premiums. In the event that you were severely injured, it is likely that you would have medical bills that could exceed $50,000 to $100,000. Some people are injured badly enough in truck accidents that their medical bills exceed $1 million. For the unfortunate few, the medical bills can exceed the one million dollar mark and leave them in a destitute stage where bankruptcy may be the only option. This may be avoided by carrying high levels of uninsured and underinsured motorist coverage benefits.

A truck driver or trucking company that is underinsured at the time of an accident may not have sufficient coverage to compensate you for your medical and economic losses. Some of the smaller trucking companies take out low-level policies, with maximum coverage of $300,000. Given the rising price of medical treatment and prescriptions, it does not take that substantial of an injury to pass the $300,000 mark. Some states require individuals to have underinsured motorist coverage, which is different from uninsured motorist coverage. This coverage would protect you in the event that you were in an accident with an underinsured motorist. You can speak to a knowledgeable insurance agent or your state's insurance commissioner to determine whether your state requires a certain level of underinsured motorist coverage.

In the event that you have underinsured motorist coverage, you can buy higher levels of coverage. Underinsured motorist coverage is defined differently in different states. In some states, the underinsured motorist coverage is stacked on top of the amount of coverage of the driver that hit you in the full amount of the underinsured motorist coverage. In other states, the law has been interpreted to mean that the underinsured motorist coverage is only the difference between the level of coverage of the driver that hit you, and whatever coverage you have. For example, if the truck driver had $300,000 of coverage and you have $1 million of underinsured motorist coverage and your damages met or exceeded one million dollars, you would have an additional $700,000 of coverage. This is dependent upon having actual compensatory damages that meet and exceed the one million dollar level. Simply purchasing a certain amount of coverage does not mean that your damages will be that same amount.

Uninsured and underinsured motorist benefits come into play quite frequently in circumstances where a truck driver or co-driver is injured by another vehicle that caused a collision, regardless of whether that other vehicle is a truck, tractor-trailer, or automobile. In those circumstances, if the motor carrier that the driver works for has not rejected the highest limits of coverage, the truck driver may be able to get additional underinsured motorist benefits from the vehicle that he was operating. Underinsured motorist coverage for a truck driver who is injured by another vehicle is an area of the law that involves many complexities in determining whether or not a driver and/or co-driver can obtain coverage through the insurance on the truck or tractor-trailer. In these circumstances, the services of a skilled trucking attorney who has an understanding of insurance law may be necessary.

Congressional Attempts to Increase the Minimum Financial Liability Requirements for Motor Carriers

On July 19, 2013, US Representative Matt Cartwright, a democrat from Pennsylvania, introduced the Safe and Fair Environment on Highways Achieved through Underwriting Levels Act. This bill was known as HR 2730 or the Safe Haul bill. This bill sought to raise the minimum liability limit for motor carriers from $750,000 to $4.42 million, with future escalation clauses as medical expenses continue to rise. The current minimum insurance level standard was established by Congress in 1980. The bill was referred to the House Committee on Transportation and Infrastructure.

The House voted to block the bill on June 10, 2014. The 214–212 vote was largely along party lines, with 210 republicans and only four democrats voting in favor. The bill was introduced because of a finding by the FMCSA that concluded in a report to Congress that the current minimum financial responsibility limits for the commercial motor vehicle industry are inadequate to meet the costs of many crashes because of rising medical costs. The FMCSA was concerned that the minimum limits had not been raised in more than thirty years.

The final report by the FMCSA was titled, "Examining the Appropriateness of the Current Financial Responsibility and Security Requirements for Motor Carriers, Brokers and Freight Forwarders–Report to Congress." This report was as a direct result of an executive summary and order by President Obama that resulted from a law called Moving Ahead for Progress in the Twenty-first Century Act. (MAP-21; P.L. 112-141). That law directed a sector of the USDOT to issue a report to the Senate Committee on Commerce, Science, and Transportation and the House Committee on Transportation and Infrastructure on the appropriateness of the current minimum financial responsibility requirements for motor carriers of property and passengers, as well as current bond and insurance requirements for freight forwarders and brokers.

This law came about because the legislative history for minimum insurance requirements on commercial motor vehicles indicated that Congress recognized decades ago that truck accident costs would change over time. It had been assumed that the DOT would periodically examine the levels of accident costs and make adjustments as necessary. The FMCSA determined that the current financial responsibility minimum limits of coverage were due for reevaluation. They formed a rulemaking team to evaluate the appropriate level of financial responsibility. In doing so, they reviewed the Motor Carrier Act of 1935, which is known as P.L. 74-255. This early law directed that no certificate or permit shall be issued to a motor carrier, unless that carrier complied with reasonable rules and regulations as the interstate commerce commission prescribe for the protection of the general public.

The next applicable law is the Motor Carrier Act of 1980. The MCA set the minimum financial responsibility level at $750,000 for the transportation of property and $5 million for the transportation of certain hazardous materials. The MCA includes a section that ties the amount of liability coverage to the fitness of the carrier to operate in interstate commerce as it relates to safety. While this particular study found that major catastrophic motor carrier-related crashes are relatively rare, occurring at the approximate rate of about 3,300 out of every 330,000 crashes per year, the same study found that the medical costs for severe and critical injury crashes can easily exceed $1 million. The analysis revealed two categories of injury crashes, which were labeled severe and critical.

The FMCSA study also found that insurance premiums had declined in real terms since the 1980s. In other words, the real value of insurance premiums or inflation-adjusted premiums had declined. The study found that the current insurance limits do not adequately cover catastrophic crashes, mainly because of increased medical costs. The report also found that the decreasing value of the current minimum levels of financial responsibilities effectively removed the function of insurance in covering catastrophic crashes. This is because from 1985 to 2013, the medical Consumer Price Index or CPI increased at a significantly higher rate than the Core Consumer Price Index. A table was created showing the necessary amounts of coverage to adjust for inflation. The table recommended that the 2013 inflation-adjusted liability limit for medical CPI established a much higher need for liability coverage minimum limits to be increased to reflect the following:

CARRIER TYPE	2013 INFLATION-ADJUSTED LIABILTY LIMIT MEDICAL CPI
General Freight	$3,188,250
HM (Low)	$4,251,000
HM (High)	$21,255,000
Small Bus	$6,376,500
Large Bus	$21,255,000

The study found the comprehensive data on premiums that motor carriers would incur to meet higher coverage limits was not readily available. The study focused mainly on freight carriers, but was also applicable to passenger and hazardous materials carriers. The study followed many significant multiple-fatality or multiple-victim crashes, such as a rollover near Sherman, Texas, in 2008 where seventeen passenger fatalities occurred. They studied another rollover crash in Victoria, Texas, in 2008, which resulted in one fatality and forty-six injuries.

They studied another rollover crash near Williams, California, in 2012 where nine passengers died. The ultimate conclusion of the study was that the current minimum financial responsibility level for motor carriers of property, hazardous materials, and passengers were established in the 1980s. Over the past twenty-nine years of insurance premiums declining, and given the decreasing real value of the current minimum financial responsibility levels, the current levels cannot effectively cover catastrophic crashes because medical and other crash-related costs have increased significantly. The study concluded that the legislative history of the federal minimum insurance requirements strongly suggests that Congress recognized that the crash costs would change. It also concluded that the FMCSA determined that the present financial responsibility minimums are inadequate to fully cover the cost of some crashes. In other words, the minimum insurance limits were inadequate to cover catastrophic injuries.

Obviously, the trucking industry fought this bill with fierce lobbying efforts. The trucking industry won and the motoring public lost. The FMCSA study found that catastrophic motor carrier crashes that result in costs over $1 million do happen. While these severe catastrophic accidents may be a lower percentage of the overall crashes, when they occur, people's lives are shattered forever.

The authors reviewed studies from The Pacific Institute for Research and Evaluation (PIRE). PIRE fought the bill, arguing that truck crashes already result in too high an amount of awards. The Trucking Alliance, however, concluded that the $750,000 limit is an inadequate amount of insurance coverage for 42 percent of crashes and it backed higher limits. The American Trucking Association (ATA) fought the bill. The ATA study argued that there was only a 1.4 percent chance of a claim exceeding $500,000. The problem with the self-policing studies by the trucking industry is that they are funded and intentionally skewed to make the public believe that truck accident victims are being compensated fairly. Statistical analysts are able to pick raw data from different sources so that it skews to a preconceived result. This is similar to the medical industry, where a drug manufacturer will perform a blind placebo study and skew the findings to get the result it wants to sell the drug on the open market and get FDA approval, while other studies in the European market will have completely different results, indicating the same drug is dangerous and kills a statistically high percentage of patients. Experts and mathematicians in this day and age can create a model that will say anything they want it to say. This is a very unfortunate reality given the present manner in which industry fights government regulation.

A recent crash occurred in the state of Kansas, where the trucking company only had four trucks. The total coverage for the trucks was $1 million per occurrence. When this particular truck driver failed to maintain an appropriate lane of travel and forced a mother with her four children into oncoming traffic, the mother was forced off of the highway into oncoming tractor-trailer traffic so she nowhere to go but to veer left off of the traveled highway. The mother was killed. One daughter was killed. Another daughter was paralyzed from the chest down. Another one of the siblings had significant lower extremity injuries with extreme scarring and underwent a number of surgeries. $1 million of coverage would not begin to fairly compensate this family with three deaths for the loss of the mother, much less the loss of the other child. The child that had the paralysis will incur tens of millions of dollars of future medical care. This unfortunate result is because the trucking industry refuses to change its view on safety. This case alone establishes a need to increase the minimum limits of financial responsibility. Cases like these occur across the United States every day.

Conclusion on Need for Increased Insurance Limits of Minimum Financial Responsibility

Given the current lame duck Congress, it is unlikely that the minimum limits of coverage will be increased until we have a new presidency. Congress is not going to help the general motoring public have a fair level of insurance coverage for catastrophic cases. Trucking victims need to have excellent skilled trucking trial lawyers help develop the case. Given the fact that many of these trucking companies are not going to voluntarily increase their insurance limits, the adept lawyer will be able to look at all additional sources of potential liability to help the catastrophically injured obtain a fair amount of recovery.

Lawyers who specialize with expertise in trucking accidents and catastrophic injuries are better suited to assist the truly injured victim. Brad Pistotnik Law is one of the firms that has dedicated years of intense study to aid and assist the victims of large truck crashes. He utilizes a team of experts that understand the Federal Motor Carrier Safety Regulations (FMCSR) as well as accident reconstruction principles and techniques. These experts are able to uniquely provide insight into a more difficult liability situation to identify those defendants who are primarily or even partially responsible for causing injury and death. The normal valuation of cases is no longer an easy task. It requires dedicated lawyers with experts who absolutely understand the entirety of the FMCSR.

12

MULTIPLE DEFENDANTS IN TRUCK ACCIDENT LITIGATION

LITIGATING A TRACTOR-TRAILER or commercial vehicle accident case is different from a normal motor vehicle simple negligence claim. Many lawyers who practice simple auto accident law are not experienced in the varying complexities that a commercial vehicle motor carrier case involves. I have seen hundreds of petitions or complaints filed by lawyers that fail to mention allegations for violations of the minimum duties set forth under the FMCSR.

Many lawyers do not bring negligent hiring, supervision, training, retention, and qualification claims. Another area that many lawyers fail to include is allegations where there is a claim that the company has a systemic failure to comply with the FMCSR and its related safety requirements. Lawyers have to be knowledgeable about the required maintenance regulations under the FMCSR. Lawyers need to be totally familiar with the FMCSR as it relates to qualifications of drivers and road tests. In almost every single tractor-trailer case, there are violations for all of these different types of causes of actions. When a lawyer fails to include them at the start of their lawsuit, that lawyer is likely giving up multiple causes of action.

Amending petitions and complaints after suit is becoming more and more difficult with the increasing changes in the federal and state Rules of Civil Procedure.

The facts of the case may lead to multiple defendants. The trucking lawyer may simply bring a claim against the truck driver under respondeat superior or vicarious liability without looking to other entities that could possibly exist, such as the tire manufacturer, the motor carrier that leased the company to start with, the vehicle manufacturer, trailer manufacturer, the loading company, and other potential defendants. There are many potential defendants in tractor-trailer cases that have catastrophic injuries. The lawyer evaluating a catastrophic injury case must immediately evaluate whom the appropriate defendant or defendants are in order to sue the appropriate parties.

The normal trucking lawyer will first evaluate the specific motor carrier safety history for violation of the FMCSR by looking at the DOT and FMCSA's website, which is located at the Safer System website under Carrier Snapshot. That study will allow the trucking lawyer to review the past two years' safety history of the particular motor carrier with an in-depth evaluation of the motor carrier's violation history of the FMCSR. Secondary to the review of the FMCSA website, the trucking lawyer will attempt to make a Freedom of Information Act (FOIA) request to the DOT to obtain a much larger database of the past history of the particular motor carrier. All of these documents are necessary for trucking safety experts to evaluate the past safety record of the motor carrier. Many motor carriers have high safety violation rates that should mandate the revocation of their operating license under the DOT. However, motor carriers spend tens of thousands of dollars with knowledgeable defense lawyers to keep their operating license by making promises to the DOT and FMCSA that they will improve their safety record. Some of the worst carriers have lost their license to operate and then filed appeals to the Federal Circuit Courts alleging that their due process and other rights have been violated.

The knowledgeable trucking lawyer must have an absolute, complete, and thorough understanding of the Motor Carrier Act (MCA), the DOT regulations, the FMCSR, and all other related industry regulatory requirements so that each particular motor carrier has a specific finding about compliance history of the FMCSR.

Once the lawyer has evaluated the actual compliance history with the FMCSR and the safety record of the company, the lawyer will look at the leasing arrangements for the truck driver and motor carrier to see if there are multiple entities to sue. The truck driver may or may not be sued independently. In many circumstances, the truck driver is left as a nonparty defendant and brought in only under the doctrines of respondeat superior and vicarious liability for tactical reasons. In other cases, an attorney may want the defendant truck driver to be involved in the case. This will usually create a conflict of interest for the motor carrier's lawyer and a second lawyer should normally be hired for the truck driver. Many unscrupulous defense lawyers choose to represent both the defendant and the motor carrier, even though they know a valid and legitimate judgment conflict of interest exists.

Once the target defendants have been identified, the lawyer must next determine whether each potential defendant has liability insurance coverage and must identify the source of that coverage. The letter of representation will typically be given to each separate defendant and each separate insurance carrier.

In this initial stage, prior to the filing of suit, it is extremely important to identify who the safety director is for each motor carrier and driver so that each safety director of each motor carrier can be given a spoliation letter. This should typically be sent at the start of the case so that the trucking company does not destroy driver logs, trip documents, bills of lading, toll receipts, fuel receipts, and other time-sensitive documents that are absolutely necessary for evaluation of whether or not the drivers have been over the maximum hours-of-service regulations under the FMCSR. This initial planning sets forth the creation of the remainder of the lawyer's theme for the case.

Drafting a Petition or Complaint For Federal or State Court

Subsequent to performing the initial investigation explained in the preceding paragraphs, the lawyer will attempt to create and draft an appropriate petition or complaint for filing in state or federal court. The lawyer must look to all potential theories of liability for different types of claims. The lawyer should evaluate simple negligence claims and then look at the more complex separate causes of action. An experienced lawyer will likely add claims for negligent hiring and retention-related claims, as well as claims that the motor carrier has violated the minimum duties of the FMCSR as it relates to safety. Additionally, the experienced trucking lawyer will typically look at claims regarding the safety programs that are used to train the drivers and whether or not they are effective or lacking in truly effective safety protocols. Many companies fail to provide new drivers with orientation, classroom training, and videotapes to instruct in safety, like those sold by the Smith System and the J.J. Keller systems of defensive driving, specifically designed for truck drivers. In order to bring these types of claims, extensive discovery is necessary. There must be a legal basis for the claim. The reason you look to the FMCSA and FMCSR Safer System carrier snapshot is so that you can evaluate preliminarily how bad the safety record of the motor carrier truly is.

When you find a motor carrier that has a high level of unsafe driving, this will give the basis for allegations for negligent qualification, hiring, training, supervision, and retention. If the motor carrier has a high violation rate for maintenance issues, then a separate type of allegation for operation of the motor carrier fleet with a poor maintenance history where equipment failure-related accidents become clearly foreseeable can be brought. Where you have a high number of reported crashes due to equipment malfunctions, tire blowouts, and other similar types of claims, there is a clear foundation for bringing this type of cause of action.

Where the actions of the motor carrier show a repeated habit and custom of unsafe driving, driver hours-of-service violations, and maintenance issues over a long period of time, it is likely that you have claims leading to wanton, willful, and perhaps malicious conduct that lead to additional claims for punitive damages. When this evidence exists, the trucking lawyer will normally be required to show that the company has ratified the conduct of their employees, which includes the drivers, dispatch people, supervising managers, and safety directors, either expressly or implied. It is often difficult to show an express ratification. Some lawyers will look to evidence that a motor carrier has simply turned a blind eye to safety by failing to utilize disciplinary programs with the three-strike rule. These reckless and careless motor carriers will allow bad drivers to continue to drive with safety violations, traffic violations, accidents, injuries, and damage to human beings and property without ever having the driver reprimanded, retrained, or terminated. The reason this loose disciplinary treatment of drivers exists is because the transportation industry as a whole is growing and there is a need for drivers. The entire transportation industry has a high turnover rate for drivers, so they tend to turn a blind eye to the bad drivers because of the difficulty in getting new drivers and training those drivers.

Once this secondary evaluation has been done, the lawyer is ready to file the appropriate petition or complaint in court.

13

DETERMINING YOUR TARGET DEFENDANTS TO SUE

THINKING THROUGH THE above criteria and analysis, the experienced trucking lawyer will hopefully be able to target the appropriate defendants at the start of the case. Sometimes certain defendants are not learned of until after discovery has taken place. In these instances, the lawyer will typically move to amend to add a new defendant. The court may or may not grant the amendment of a motion to add a new defendant. The best practices rule states that each and every defendant should be identified at the start of the case before filing suit. One of the complications with trying to identify all of the known entities is that the trucking companies and motor carriers do not willingly give up information.

Once the suit is filed in court, the trucking company defense attorneys will try to hold back as much discovery as they can. Many of the bigger trucking defense firms will file multiple motions for summary judgment, motions to strike, or motions to dismiss in an effort to thwart the plaintiff's attorney from seeking the appropriate remedies from all potential defendants for all potential different causes of action.

One of the main concerns for trial lawyers is to identify only the truly necessary parties and sue only those necessary parties. There is an opposite rule that applies to cases where a lawyer chooses to sue too many defendants at once. Given the current trend in litigation, which is in a decline, it has to be understood that the defense lawyers, who get paid for defending a case, will hold onto a case as long as humanly possible. The more lawyers you have on the case, the more extensive and obnoxious the theories of defense will be. A good trial lawyer will try to minimize the number of defendants and attorneys to a manageable amount for the case to still have a successful resolution.

In order to determine the number of parties to sue, the lawyer has to look at the damages of the particular plaintiff. Obviously, a plaintiff who has a level of damages of $100,000 to $200,000, as compared to a plaintiff who has damages at $1 million or above, would lead to a different determination on how many defendants to sue. A general rule can be stated that with catastrophic injury cases, it is normally better to look for all the target defendants at the start of the case and bring claims against all defendants that have liability insurance.

The expert truck lawyer will be able to rapidly assess and determine the correct parties to sue given the determination of damages of each particular case and client.

Minimizing the Number of Defendants as an Advantage Point

One of the biggest mistakes a lawyer can make is to name too many defendants in a lawsuit at one time. This leads to an aggregation of defense lawyers who strategize against your plaintiff's counsel to defeat the entire case. Thus, it is essential that your lawyer sue only the defendants with real fault. This is one of the places where there is a Catch-22. The lawyer that does not sue enough defendants has a problem that requires amendment of pleadings. On the other hand, the lawyer who sues too many defendants will face a barrage of motions to dismiss and motions for summary judgment. Those motions are the basic funding for defense firms. Defense firms love to have motions for summary judgment because of the substantial number of hours it takes to write and argue these particular types of tactical motions. Multiple defense lawyers arguing multiple motions to defend is like a feeding frenzy of piranhas going after a school of minnows. The defense lawyers feed off the case until it is concluded, and they know when to give up.

Generally, the experienced trucking lawyer will plead a sufficient number of alternative causes of action, such that the case cannot be thrown out with a motion for summary judgment. A motion for summary judgment is a motion that sets forth a series of factual statements and argues that there is no issue of fact for the jury to determine, so that the court should dismiss the case as a matter of law. Lawyers who file simplistic pleadings without alternative causes of action can find themselves dismissed out of court rapidly.

The goal of the plaintiff's attorney fighting for a trucking accident victim is to plead the correct alternative causes of action that will sustain the case through motions to dismiss and motions for summary judgment and ultimately to presentation to the jury. The most important rule for your trucking lawyer to follow is to write a petition or complaint that will make it before the jury without being dismissed.

In the event that your case loses one of its alternative causes of action, you can still proceed to the jury with the remaining causes of action. This type of pleading practice is known as aggressive, proactive, and preemptive litigation, which is designed to eliminate the chance of being dismissed out of court. When a pleading is correctly pled with all appropriate allegations for all appropriate causes of action, the chances of being kicked out of court on some type of dismissal motion are greatly minimized.

Choose the valid and legitimate target defendants with valid and legitimate allegations against them for negligent and wanton actions and your case will have a great chance of success.

Early Settlement with one of Several Defendants May Have a Negative Impact on the Remainder of Your Case
In all litigation, there are times where multiple defendants are being sued together and one of the defendants decides to try and settle and buy out of the litigation at an early juncture. This presents a unique problem for the trial lawyer. Once you have settled with a single defendant and leave remaining defendants in the litigation, those other defendants will instantly attempt to shift all arguments of liability against the settling defendant. Sometimes an injured victim must settle in order to help pay for medical costs from their injuries, and other economic losses suffered after a catastrophic accident in order to obtain continuing medical care and not end up in bankruptcy court. That is a tactical decision that has to be made case by case and determined on the independent facts of each unique case.

When you settle with one defendant, you may potentially kill the remaining claims against other remaining defendants. Thus, it is extremely important to analyze the levels of comparative fault of each particular defendant. Some states look at contributory fault, while others use comparative fault analysis. There are many different rules in different states, which make it exceedingly difficult to settle with one defendant and still have remaining claims against the others.

The introduction of settlement documents, releases, and other dismissal documents as evidence before the jury at time of trial may present another substantial problem that must be thought about prior to settlement. An example of the problem posed in this hypothetical scenario is the set of facts where the main defendant with the most fault settles out the case.

The remaining defendants will do everything in their power to make certain that the jury is allowed to hear that the other defendants settled. Different states have different rules on the admissibility of this evidence. No matter what state you are in, it is extremely important that you have those documents drafted in such a manner as to expect their introduction before the jury with as little being said about the level of fault of the settling defendant as possible. In other words, if a lawyer for the defense admits fault or admits some type of negligent action and those words are set forth in a settlement release, or another pleading that could potentially be placed in front of the jury at time of trial, it is highly dangerous to the injured plaintiff's remaining case.

In some circumstances, it is very important to settle with the defendant who admits fault. The lawyer has to realize that there is a substantial effect on any claims against remaining defendants. In many cases, the settlement with one defendant sets the standard for the remaining case and will create a barrier against proving claims against the remaining defendants. For these reasons, the lawyer must carefully analyze whether it is wise to settle with one defendant and leave remaining defendants. Most attorneys are aware that once you settle with one defendant, the jury may come to a conclusion that the settling defendant was at fault and the remaining defendants have little or no fault. These are tactical decisions that must be made with the lawyer and the client. The decision to settle is usually based upon the amount of settlement monies being offered and the analysis of the remaining fault of the defendants who stay in the litigation.

In order to reach a conclusion as to how to proceed in this scenario of settlement with one out of multiple defendants, it is important to review the rules of evidence in the particular state where the suit has been filed. If the case is being tried in federal court under the Federal Rules of Evidence (FRE), then remember that federal courts will not apply state procedural rules, but will apply state substantive laws of the particular state. If you are in federal court, the lawyer will need to analyze both state and federal law in that jurisdiction. The risks of settlement with one defendant have to be fully understood before agreeing to settle. There are times when it is too risky to settle with one defendant, where it is better to proceed to trial against all defendants to allow the jury to assess different fault findings against each defendant.

When you have sued a driver and the motor carrier that the driver works for, it is difficult to settle with the driver and leave any remaining claims against the motor carrier. The reason for this is that in many states there are laws that have an effect on a settlement with the employer or employee or master or servant. When you release one, but not the other, the release may have the same effect and may completely release both parties at one time through effect of law. There are many precarious rules to be concerned with when you have multiple defendants and attempt to settle with one. The lawyer and the client must carefully analyze the effect of settlement with only one defendant before agreeing to a final settlement with the particular defendants offering money.

14

A Comprehensive Discussion of The Federal Motor Carrier Safety Regulations To Understand Safety Compliance Rules For Motor Carriers

Lawyers pursuing a claim for bodily injuries against a motor carrier should be aware of the unique characteristics of the FMCSR. Many lawyers unfamiliar with the FMSCR will file the usual motor vehicle petition with a set of ordinary negligence allegations, claiming only respondeat superior liability for the truck driver. The lawyer who fails to use the FMCSR is limiting his or her client's ability to establish negligence for many specific regulatory requirements. The requirements are broad and apply not only to the driver but also to the motor carrier. Their regulatory effect places obligations on the carrier to properly hire, qualify, train, monitor, supervise, and direct the driver. In order to properly litigate these claims, lawyers must have a working knowledge of the regulations and their applicability to a specific set of facts.

In addition to the FMSCR, the regulations commencing at 49 C.F.R. § 365–399 are useful regulations that are related to the FMCSR. These regulations commence with regulations on the Rules Governing a Motor Carrier's Application for Operating Authority under the DOT. Lawyers practicing in this area should be familiar with all regulations from 49 C.F.R.§ 365–399 in order to have a complete understanding of the laws applicable to truck drivers and motor carriers.

I. The Fmcsr Sets The Applicable Standard Of Care

The FMCSR are located at 49 C.F.R. § 390 *et seq.* Authority for the FMCSR is found in the Motor Carrier Act, PL 96–296, 1980 S 2245 and PL 96–296, July 1, 1980, 94 Stat 793. The MCA provides that, "a motor carrier shall provide safe and adequate service, equipment, and facilities." 49 U.S.C. § 14101(a). It also provides that, "A carrier...is liable for damages sustained by a person as a result of an act or omissions of that carrier...in violation of this part." 49 U.SC. § 14704(a)(2).

The FMCSR set the applicable standard of care. Claims can be alternatively made. The trucking lawyer should write allegations and claims using the FMCSR as the minimum standard of care in the trucking industry.

Their applicability in most states is usually codified through local state statutes and administrative regulations, making them applicable to both intrastate and interstate commerce.

The FMCSR requirements establish a minimum standard of care for the evaluation of driver qualifications. The regulations also provide that trucking companies may enforce "more stringent requirements relating to safety of operation" than the general requirements found in the FMCSR, 49 C.F.R. § 390.3(d), and may require driver applicants to provide information in addition to that required to be disclosed by the regulations. 49 C.F.R. § 391.21(c) (2000). *Cassara v. DAC Services, Inc.,* 276 F.3d 1210, 1212, 1213 (C.A. 10 (Okla.) 2002))

"A motor carrier's duty to ensure that a driver is physically qualified is a continuing one." *Yellow Freight System, Inc. v. Amestoy,* 736 F. Supp. 44, 48, 49, 50 (D. Vt. 1990). "A driver who is disqualified shall not drive a commercial motor vehicle. An employer shall not knowingly allow, require, permit, or authorize a driver who is disqualified to drive a commercial motor vehicle." 49 C.F.R. § 383.51.

"Motor carrier means a for-hire motor carrier or a private motor carrier. The term includes a motor carrier's agents, officers, and representatives as well as employees **responsible for hiring, supervising, training, assigning, or dispatching** of drivers and employees concerned with the installation, inspection, and maintenance of motor vehicle equipment and/or accessories." 49 C.F.R. § 390.5.

"The rules in this part establish minimum qualifications for persons who drive commercial motor vehicles, as for, or on behalf of motor carriers. The rules in this part also establish minimum duties of motor carriers with respect to the qualification of their drivers." 49 C.F.R. § 391.1(a).

These regulations obligate the trucking company to protect the motoring public. The trucking company typically will be in a position of obligatory monitoring of all drivers for compliance with the FMCSR.

The regulations set forth immediately below are the main regulations that pertain to the usual trucking case. Some, but not all, may be relevant to the normal trucking case.

Regulation 49 C.F.R. § 392.3 requires that no driver shall operate a commercial motor vehicle while the driver's ability

TRUCK ACCIDENTS KILL

or alertness is so impaired or so likely to become impaired through fatigue as to make it unsafe for him to begin or continue to operate the commercial motor vehicle.

Regulation 49 C.F.R. § 395.3 requires that no motor carrier shall permit and no driver shall drive more than eleven cumulative hours in a fourteen-hour period following ten consecutive hours off duty. It further requires that no driver shall drive after having been on duty sixty hours in any seven consecutive days if the motor carrier does not operate every day of the week. If the motor carrier operates every day of the week then no driver shall drive after having been on duty seventy hours in any period of eight consecutive days. The prior daily hour rule was known as the ten-hour rule and required eight hours off, in contrast to the modified rule allowing eleven hours of driving but requiring ten hours of off-duty time before driving again.

Regulation 49 C.F.R. § 395.8 requires that every driver shall record his duty status in duplicate for each twenty-four-hour period of duty and shall record it on a specific grid. Failure to complete the record of duty activities, failing to preserve a record, or making a false record is a violation of these regulations. All entries relating to driver's duty status must be legible and in the driver's own handwriting. The total mileage driven during the twenty-four-hour period shall be recorded on the form containing the driver's duty status record. The driver shall certify to the correctness of the information recorded.

Regulation 49 C.F.R. § 391.11(a) requires that an employer, "not require or permit a person to drive a commercial motor vehicle unless that person is qualified to drive a commercial motor vehicle under 49 C.F.R. 391.11(a). (See the discussion below on driver qualification for further explanation.)

Regulation 49 C.F.R. § 391.23 requires that the motor carrier make an inquiry into the driver's driving record during the preceding three years and must make a written record with respect to each past employer who was contacted. The record must include the past employer's name and address, the date he or she was contacted, and his or her comments with respect to the driver. This includes an inquiry into each state where the driver has driven a commercial motor vehicle in the past three years prior to employment in the new job with the new motor carrier. This requires more than simply doing a background check. It requires that the employer actually make a good faith effort to document the background check.

Regulation 49 C.F.R. § 383.35 requires that a driver must provide his employment history for ten years preceding the date the application is submitted for hire. It must include the names and addresses of the applicant's previous employers, the dates of hire with the previous employers, the reasons for leaving, and be certified that it is true and correct. The applicant must be informed that the employer will use this information for investigation of the applicant's work history.

Regulation 49 C.F.R. § 383.1(b) prohibits a commercial motor vehicle driver from having more than one commercial motor vehicle driver's license and requires that a driver possess and demonstrate safe driving skills, which include proper visual search methods, appropriate use of signals, speed control for weather and traffic conditions, and ability to position the motor vehicle correctly when changing lanes or turning.

Regulation 49 C.F.R. § 383.111 requires that a driver have knowledge of safe operating regulations, including the effects of fatigue, safety systems knowledge, basic knowledge of basic control maneuvers, and basic information on hazard perception, and when and how to make emergency maneuvers. This includes knowledge of the effect of fatigue. The driver must have knowledge of night operation, including issues concerning vision, glare, fatigue, and inexperience. The driver must have knowledge about how to drive in extreme driving conditions, such as bad weather, hot weather, mountain driving, and other conditions that make the operation of the commercial motor vehicle more difficult. The driver must understand skid control maneuvers to help avoid accidents and hazards. This includes techniques on how to make a recovery of the tractor-trailer after a skid where the CMV becomes out of control. The driver must be knowledgeable in proper braking techniques. The driver must be knowledgeable about hazardous materials and their effect on humans and the motoring public.

Regulation 49 C.F.R. § 383.110 requires that a driver shall have the knowledge and skills necessary to operate a commercial motor vehicle safely.

Regulation 49 C.F.R. § 390.11 establishes a duty that the motor carrier require its driver to observe and follow the safety regulations. Where the motor carrier is likewise the driver, then the driver is bound to this same duty of care.

Regulation 49 C.F.R. § 392.4 requires that no driver shall be on duty and possess or be under the influence of illegal drugs generally described as amphetamine or any formulation thereof which are more commonly referred to as "pep pills" or "bennies." The prohibition extends to any narcotic or a derivative of any narcotic.

Regulation 49 C.F.R. § 392.5 requires that no driver shall be under the influence of alcohol within four hours before going on duty, operating, or having physical control of a commercial motor vehicle.

Regulation 49 C.F.R. § 392.22 requires that whenever a commercial motor vehicle is stopped upon the traveled portion of a highway or the shoulder of a highway for any cause other than necessary traffic stops, the driver of the stopped commercial motor vehicle shall immediately activate the vehicular hazard warning signal flashers and continue the flashing until the driver places the warning devices required by this regulation into place.

Regulation 49 C.F.R. § 392.22(b)(2)(iii) requires stopped or parked tractor-trailers to place hazard warning flashers, triangles, fuses, or other warning devices in a business or residential district when street or highway lighting is insufficient to make a commercial motor vehicle clearly discernible at a distance of five hundred feet to persons on the highway.

The DOT writes interpretations of the regulations that can be found in the Federal Register. These interpretations are useful for determining the applicability of a specific regulation to a particular case.

These are but a few of the many regulations that apply to the average trucking case. The applicability of each regulation to a given case will depend upon the facts. In many cases, it will be useful to employ an expert with a background in the trucking industry, especially in the area of safety. More often than not, you will be facing a motion for summary judgment or motion in limine, seeking an order of the court eliminating these regulatory claims from the case.

II. Fatigue and Hours of Service Limits

Probably the single most significant claim that can be made against drivers and the companies they work for is the claim of driver fatigue. 49 C.F.R. § 392.3 requires that no driver shall operate a commercial motor vehicle while the driver's ability or alertness is so impaired or so likely to become impaired through fatigue as to make it unsafe for him to begin or continue to operate the commercial motor vehicle. 49 C.F.R. § 395.3 has recently been modified. The regulation on maximum hours has been modified from the old ten-hour rule to the new rule that no driver shall drive more than eleven cumulative hours following ten consecutive hours off duty. This regulation additionally applies to the maximum hours a driver may drive in any eight-day period. It is limited to seventy hours.

Drivers are notorious for violating these regulations by driving in excess of the period allowed by law. Some drivers routinely carry two sets of logbooks. They keep a partially completed logbook to show to law enforcement when stopped and a second set of books with their actual driving time.

In one particular case I tried in Federal Court in Wichita, the driver drove from the border of California/New Mexico into Kansas. His seventy hours expired when the driver approached the town of Texhoma in Oklahoma. Rather than cease driving, the driver falsely logged sleep time and indicated on the log that the last place of destination for the date was Texhoma, Oklahoma. In actuality, the driver continued to drive into Wichita, Kansas, for an additional five hours, making the total time approximately seventy-five hours. The false logs become an admissible piece of evidence that can be used to establish fatigue, negligence, wanton conduct, fraud, and a lack of credibility.

Many lawyers who do not routinely handle trucking cases will attempt to settle a case via the usual route, by settlement brochure. A major problem with waiting is that the trucking companies will retain their driver's logs for a period of only six months. Many trucking companies will use an outside vendor to audit their drivers' logs for compliance with the FMCSR maximum hours-of-service requirements. In those instances, the actual log will be scanned into the software program and the original log will be destroyed. The programs are often designed to automatically delete the drivers' logs at the expiration of six months. If the trucking lawyer has not already filed suit and sought discovery early on following the accident, then the necessary evidence to establish fatigue may be lost.

One manner of avoiding prompt filing of suit is to send out a spoliation letter placing the company on notice of your claim and requesting that they not destroy necessary evidence. In that event, the letter should be by certified mail to their safety director, vice president of risk management, or some other officer in the company. The better procedure is to institute litigation shortly after the accident.

In addition to the claim of driver fatigue, you can bring allegations that the trucking company's safety protocols and procedures or lack thereof result in the driver being forced to drive excessive hours to meet the company's profit needs.

Most medium-sized companies to larger companies utilize satellite-tracking services like Qualcomm. Qualcomm allows the trucking company to have satellite positions on all trucks in their fleet. Many trucking companies will use this to determine if the truck will be late on arrival. Fleet managers will routinely receive computerized notices from the company's satellite tracking system informing them that a certain driver or tractor is going to be hours or days late on reaching their point of destination.

Most companies do not utilize the Qualcomm software, which will warn them when a driver is close to running out of hours for the day or eight-day period. They choose not to use this software because of the increased risk of liability for allowing their drivers to operate in a fatigued state.

By using appropriate written and deposition discovery, you can establish in many cases that the trucking company provides financial incentives to fleet managers for keeping delivery on time. These incentives make the fleet managers push the drivers to meet company goals. In turn, the driver's falsify logs in order to meet company deadlines. This blind-eye approach to safety provides the basis for claims for wanton and intentional misconduct under punitive damage theories. Likewise, it provides the basis for claims of ratification from the failure to act to prevent egregious violation of the maximum hours-of-service rules.

Establishing fatigue will usually, but not always require the use of an expert to inspect the driver's logs, log audits, shipping manifest documents, trip receipts, gas receipts, bills of lading, and hours-of-service records.

Discovery should seek any and all documents created in reference to the FMCSR, Part 395, including, but not limited to, driver's record of duty status or drivers' daily logs, time worked cards or other time work records or summaries, administrative driver's record of duty status or log audits and/ or seventy/sixty-hour log audits or summaries, along with any records or reports of violations or any otherwise described documents advising any of the defendant's drivers for hours-of-service violations.

Discovery should further seek all receipts for any trip expenses or purchases made by the driver or his co-driver during a trip regardless of type of purchase, such as fuel, weighing of vehicles, food, lodging, equipment maintenance, repair, or equipment cleaning, special or oversize permits, bridge and/ or toll roads, loading or unloading cost, and all other receipts regardless of the type of objects or services purchased. This will include cargo pickup or delivery documents prepared by any of the driver or carrier defendants, transportation brokers, involved shippers or receivers, motor carriers operations/dispatch personnel, or other persons or organizations relative to the cargo transported and the operations of the defendant trucking company.

Once you have the totality of the logs, shipping documents, trip documents, and other necessary documentation, the driver's trip and hours can be reconstructed. Mileage can be computed through PC Miler or other similar software programs. The logs may show a different number of hours than the trip documents, which are time-stamped. Mileage can be calculated using points of reference, stops, locations, fuel stops, toll receipts, and time-stamps analyzing how fast the truck driver would have to be driving to get from one point to another. This analysis almost always leads to a different conclusion than what is actually recorded on the driver logs.

The routine appearance of compliance with the maximum hours-of-service rules does not mean that the driver was in compliance with the FMCSR. Proving the noncompliance can be tiring and frustrating. Many defense attorneys will object to production of the documentation until a motion to compel has been filed. Written discovery will only rarely turn up all of the necessary documentation. To establish fatigue, you must depose necessary witnesses, including the driver, safety director, fleet supervisors, risk management personnel, log audit personnel, and operations personnel. Often, more can be learned from the direct fleet supervisors than from the skilled upper management, who are adept at testifying in depositions. In other words, start with low-level employees and then work your way up the food chain until you get to the VP of Safety and Operations. You can utilize the lower-level employees' depositions that tend to be more truthful in order to get an admission against interest out of the upper-level vice presidents and other chief officers.

Fatigue claims can prove to be an independent source of negligence against the trucking companies. These claims, when established properly, will lead to a case with substantially more value.

III. Choice of Forum

Your choice of forum may be the single most important decision you make in the case. Many trucking cases occur in rural settings where a jury panel may end up being comprised of rural juries who award much less than juries in larger venues.

In analyzing jurisdiction and forum choices, the out-of-state trucking company and driver will always provide a basis for federal diversity jurisdiction. This will normally allow a case to be filed in Federal Court to get away from a smaller farming area. You can typically seek jurisdiction where the defendant driver resides, or where the defendant motor carrier has its principal place of business or transacts a majority of its business.

When a driver is an out-of-state driver and is supervised in another state or dispatched from another state, this can provide an alternate venue. In one case that occurred near Garden City, Kansas, the driver of the motor carrier lived in a Dallas suburb. He was dispatched from Texas. His return destination was Texas. Fleet managers monitored the driver from out-of-state locations. In that particular case, the court applied Texas substantive law, which eliminated any cap on pain and suffering from Kansas, which has one of the most conservative caps on noneconomic damages in the nation. While this effect may not occur in every case, where the client has substantial damages, consideration of out-of-state forums should be given great weight and consideration.

IV. Negligent Hiring, Qualification, Training, Supervision, and Retention

The use of independent tort claims for negligent hiring, qualification, training, supervision, and retention provides a basis for eliminating defense counsel's admission of fault to minimize the more egregious facts in a case. Skilled defense counsel will attempt to eliminate liability considerations by the jury, thereby allowing the jury to focus only on damages. Depending upon the case, it may be more desirous to have liability determined by the jury. By adding these independent tort claims to your case, you can strengthen the case and prevent this common defense strategy from succeeding.

The majority of states follow the *McHaffie rule*, which prevents a plaintiff from bringing claims against the carrier under the doctrine of respondeat superior and then bringing additional independent tort claims for negligent hiring, training, supervising, and retention. The rule in McHaffie is that once an employer admits liability under respondeat superior, the plaintiff may not proceed against the employer on a negligent entrustment or negligent hiring or supervision theory. *Marquis v. State Farm,* 265 Kan. 317, 334, 961 P.2d 1213 (1998); *see McHaffie v. Bunch,* 891 S.W. 2d 822 (Mo.

1995) That rule of law is totally inapplicable to a case applying substantive law from the state of Kansas. Several other states have shifted away from the *McHaffie rule*.

The Kansas Supreme Court analyzed why Kansas does not follow the majority rule in *McHaffie, Id*. Subsequently, the case of *Patterson v. Dahlsten,* 130 F. Supp.2d 1228 (D. Kan. 2000) analyzed *McHaffie* and why Kansas has led away from this prior rule of law. The *Patterson* court analyzed the change in Kansas's law from the ruling interpreting the *Marquis* case. The *Marquis* decision recognized that the majority of jurisdictions preclude a plaintiff from proceeding against an employee on a negligent hiring, supervision, or entrustment theory where liability under respondeat superior has been admitted, so as to avoid confusion, wasted judicial resources, and the introduction of inflammatory evidence irrelevant to any contested issue. The court found that other jurisdictions, including Kansas, have found that an admission that the employee was acting within the scope of his or her employment does not preclude an action for both respondeat superior and negligent entrustment or negligent hiring, retention, or supervision. (*See Kansas State Bank & Tr. Co. v. Specialized Transp. Services, Inc.,* 249 Kan. 348, 819 P.2d 587 (1991); *Quinonez v. Andersen,* 144 Ariz. 193, 696 P.2d 1342 (1984); *Lim v. Interstate Sys. Steel Div., Inc.,* 435 N.W.2d 830 (Minn.App.1989); *Clark v. Stewart,* 126 Ohio St. 263, 185 N.E. 71 (1933)).

After evaluating the *Marquis* decision, the *Patterson* court ruled,

...in Kansas, the torts of negligent hiring, retention, or supervision are torts "distinct from respondeat superior," as they are "not derivative of the employee's negligence." *Id*. at 1225. "Liability is not imputed, but instead runs directly from the employer to the person injured."

Id. See also, <u>Miller v. Dillard's Inc., 47 F.Supp.2d 1294, 1299 (D.Kan.1999)</u> **("Even if the employer admits the employee was acting within the scope of his or her employment, the plaintiff may still bring an action for both respondeat superior and negligent entrustment or negligent hiring, retention, or supervision.")** [internal quotation and citation omitted]; <u>*Mart v. Dr. Pepper Co., 923 F. Supp. 1380, 1389 (D.Kan.1996)*</u> **("Liability for negligent supervision and retention is not vicarious liability under the doctrine of respondeat superior, but is direct liability....")**. Therefore, the Kansas court held that "State Farm's admission in this case that Jerry Auck was an employee acting within the scope of his employment at the time of the accident does not prohibit the plaintiffs from maintaining an action based on claims of negligent hiring, retention, or supervision. *Id.* The Kansas Supreme Court's decision in *Marquis* clearly negates Dahlsten's argument in support of its motion for summary judgment. Applying Kansas law, the court finds that **Dahlsten's concession of respondeat superior liability does not preclude plaintiff from proceeding on separate claims against Dahlsten for negligent hiring, training, retention, or supervision."** 130 F.Supp.2d at 1232, 1233. [footnotes omitted] [emphasis supplied]

The legal analysis above illustrates why counsel should add the separate tort claims in addition to liability under respondeat superior. These direct liability claims will enhance the injured party's legal position. The additional claims are each separate and distinct causes of action. The driver's negligence is just one small part of the overall case.

Negligent hiring claims arise from the motor carrier's failure to conduct adequate background checks. Many motor carriers will use DAC Services. This is a service throughout the trucking industry that has a system for driver background verification. The members of this service report accidents, terminations, and other relevant information to the service. For a fee, the hiring carrier can conduct a quick and inexpensive background check. Some carriers will simply rely on this service rather than conduct any individual inquiry. Due to the high turnover rate of drivers in the trucking industry, which can be over 100 percent in a year, the reporting companies inform DAC Services if the driver is available for rehire. When the trucking companies find the notation that a driver is not eligible to be rehired or is eligible to be rehired only after a review, this should provide a red flag that the driver has a poor history. Failing to conduct further inquiry into the driver's background, or hiring the driver in this circumstance, may provide the basis to the jury for a finding of negligent hiring. The Tenth Circuit Court of Appeals discussed the development of the DAC stating,

As often is the case, the federal regulation of one commercial activity gave birth to another new business opportunity—in this case, the gathering and reporting of drivers' records and employment histories for a fee. DAC was formed in 1981 to exploit that opportunity, first by building a database of truck driver employment histories. Beginning in 1983, DAC offered employment histories, employee driving records, and other reports to its trucking industry members nationwide, augmenting its database with information reported by its participating employers. In its own words, DAC acts as a "file cabinet," storing employment histories on terminated drivers for over 2,500 truck lines and private carriers from across the country. Participating member employers can access the DAC database, which currently contains over four million records, to gather key employment history information. DAC advertises that its employment history files comply with the federal regulations and are accepted by the United States Department

of Transportation to satisfy Section 391.23(c) of the Federal
Motor Carrier Safety Regulations, governing investigations of
driver applicants' employment history. *Cassara*, 276 F.3d 1210,
1214 (C.A. 10 (Okla.) 2002)

49 C.F.R. 391.23 requires that the motor carrier make an
inquiry into the driver's driving record during the preceding three years and must make a written record with respect
to each past employer who was contacted. The record must
include the past employer's name and address, the date he
or she was contacted, and his or her comments with respect
to the driver. Trucking carriers often ignore this regulatory
requirement. This regulation makes it necessary to always
obtain the application of the driver. The driver's applications
should be compared to the actual driver qualification file
documents, verifying that the company actually followed the
regulation.

Negligent qualification of the driver can be established
in many different manners. 49 C.F.R. § 391.11(a) requires that
an employer, "not require or permit a person to drive a commercial motor vehicle unless that person is qualified to drive
a commercial motor vehicle under 49 C.F.R. 391.11(a) A driver
may not be permitted to drive until he has a doctor's certification indicating that he is physically qualified to drive under
this same regulation. Motor carriers are prohibited from per-
mitting any person who is not in compliance with the applicable regulations to drive a commercial motor vehicle under
this regulation. To be qualified, the driver must be medically
examined and certified as physically qualified to operate a
commercial motor vehicle. The qualification rule is "absolute," such that without qualification a driver may not drive.
Qualification requires mandatory drug testing and a motor
carrier may not allow a driver to drive until the drug testing
qualification requirement has been met. The goal of mandatory drug testing is to ensure a drug-free transportation

environment, which in turn will reduce accidents and casualties in motor carrier operations. Urinalysis is a compulsory part of the mandatory qualification procedure. Both employer and employee have an affirmative duty to ensure that only qualified drivers operate commercial motor vehicles.

Carriers may be negligent for improperly hiring and screening a driver. They may be liable for failing to medically qualify and drug test a new driver. In every case where this claim is presented, it is necessary to obtain the driver's medical background checks, drug test results, and other relevant driving history information.

Many companies will place the driver on the road before the drug test results are received. This will violate the FMCSR.

Negligent training claims arise from the regulations. 49 C.F.R. § 383.111 requires that a driver have knowledge of safe operating regulations, including the effects of fatigue, safety systems knowledge, basic knowledge of basic control maneuvers, and basic information on hazard perception, and when and how to make emergency maneuvers. 49 C.F.R. § 383.110 requires that a driver shall have the knowledge and skills necessary to operate a commercial motor vehicle safely. 49 C.F.R. § 390.11 establishes a duty that the motor carrier require its driver to observe and follow the safety regulations.

Many trucking companies simply hand a FMCSR pocketbook to the driver. They have the driver certify he has read the pocketbook and then place him on the road. These regulations are difficult for a lawyer to interpret, much less, the ordinary truck driver with a high school diploma or less. Truck drivers rarely have sufficient training to understand these far-reaching regulations on safety.

Written discovery will help counsel obtain the necessary safety protocols, manuals, bulletins, training materials, and videotapes available. Many companies will buy training videotapes from sources like J.J. Keller. Others will produce their own videotapes. Accessing and reviewing training videotapes is necessary to establish company violation of its own training protocols on safety. Some carriers will produce independent training tapes.

Independently produced training videotapes can almost always be used against the carrier to establish that they train the drivers in a completely different safety protocol than what the company actually implements. Counsel should take the time to review each and every minute of training videotapes to look for evidence contradicting management testimony. Without a doubt, the safety director, director of operations, and risk management personnel will testify on behalf of the company that the company followed proper safety protocols. Many of these executives can be proven to be lacking in credibility by using training materials produced by the company during cross-examination.

Negligent supervision can be established by proving that the carrier is monitoring and supervising their drivers' daily activities while ignoring the drivers' failure to comply with the FMCSR. (See discussion above on fatigue.) Drivers routinely call in to determine where their next delivery will be. Few dispatchers bother to inquire whether the driver has sufficient hours left to make the delivery without violating the maximum hours-of-service rules. This failure to inquire is an act of negligence that can convince the jury a carrier is lacking in safety procedures that would have helped prevent an accident.

Negligent supervision includes not only the duty to supervise but also the duty to control persons with whom the defendant has a special relationship, including the defendant's employees, or persons with dangerous propensities. *See Nero v. Kansas State University*, 253 Kan. 567, 861 P.2d 768 (1993); *C.J.W. v. State*, 253 Kan. 1, 853 P.2d 4 (1993); *Anspach v. Tomkins Industries, Inc.*, 817 F.Supp. 1499, 1519-20 (D.Kan.1993); *Kansas State Bank & Tr. Co. v. Specialized Transportation Services, Inc.*, 249 Kan. 348, 819 P.2d 587 (1991)

Negligent retention relates to the prior bad acts and omissions of the driver. The usual claim will arise where a driver has had more than one accident. The carriers, deeply in need of drivers, will continue to use bad drivers in order to meet delivery deadlines. This claim may be established by developing evidence that a motor carrier has knowledge of or ignores its driver repeatedly violating the maximum hours-of-service rules. In some instances, the motor carrier may learn that a driver has refused a drug test. If so, placing the driver back on the road may be sufficient to establish that the driver was negligently retained. These are but a few of the myriad factual scenarios that can support a claim for negligent retention.

V. Use of Experts

Expert testimony is usually necessary in trucking litigation. Trucking experts come in a variety of types. The most useful trucking experts have prior trucking industry experience as a driver, dispatcher, safety director, or all of the above. The expert will analyze the facts in the case to determine compliance with the FMCSR. The more knowledgeable experts will help aid in the creation of discovery documents to analyze the violations.

The PC Miler and Household Movers Guide are two programs that many experts use to recreate the itinerary of the driver. A map can be created by the expert to explain to the jury what route the driver took to arrive at the accident location. The expert can pinpoint the appropriate time of travel between the point of origin and destination point. Many truck drivers will travel an extraordinary amount of miles in a day. Their logs will show on the surface that they are compliant with the FMCSR. The expert can be useful to explain how the driver, if following the proper speed limits and taking required breaks, could not have driven the distance in the time stated. This, in turn, will lead to the conclusion that the logs are fabricated in an effort to comply with the maximum hours rules.

The expert will be useful in accessing DOT information on the trucking company. The expert can explain how the safety record of the company is higher than the statistical averages of all carriers nationwide. Analysis of the safety record can help establish a claim that the trucking company has a company-wide policy of ignoring safety protocols.

When seeking punitive damages, it is the expert who can provide the necessary opinion of intentional, wanton, fraudulent, or malicious acts and omissions. Many states simply require a finding that the driver or motor carrier acted with reckless disregard to the safety of others. Without the expert, it is likely that the punitive damage claims will not survive summary judgment.

An expert who was once a driver or safety director for a trucking company can provide a bird's eye view of why the trucking company violated the FMCSR, its own safety protocols, and/or acted recklessly.

Great care should be taken in picking your expert. The experts are expensive and can cost tens of thousands of dollars in additional litigation expense. Very few local trucking experts exist. The best experts will usually be from distant states where the trucking industry flourishes. They become tired of the constant patterns of safety violations and leave to become an advocate for the victims of the trucking industry. Before hiring your expert, you should satisfy yourself that he or she is knowledgeable about FMCSR and DOT compliance.

VI. Alter-Ego
You should always consider an alter-ego claim in trucking litigation. A substantial number of large carriers set up smaller corporate shells for liability protection. These parent companies will set up a lock-box system of revenue. The smaller corporations will transfer all gross income from the smaller trucking company into a central bank account. The larger parent company will pay all expenses and salaries of the smaller company

through this lock-box system. In effect, the parent retains total control over the smaller trucking company.

When suit is filed against the smaller company, the profits are in a much different range than the total gross profit of the entire group of companies. The alter-ego claim is beneficial whenever you plan to seek punitive damages. It can help increase the gross profit of the company in order to meet Kansas caps on punitive damages.

The Kansas Supreme Court applied the alter-ego doctrine to parent corporations and their subsidiaries in two separate opinions. *See Doughty v. CSX Transportation, Inc.,* 905 P. 2d 106, 109-111 (1995); *Dean Operations v. One Seventy Assoc.,* 896 P.2d 1012, 1016-1018 (1995) These authorities set out a ten-factor test, with the ultimate consideration being, "whether, from all of the facts and circumstances, it is apparent that the relationship between the parent and subsidiary is so intimate, the parent's control over the subsidiary is so dominating, and the business and the assets of the two are so mingled that recognition of the subsidiary as a distinct entity would result in an injustice to third parties." *Doughty,* 905 P.2d at 111.

In the event that punitive damages are not an issue then presentation of alter-ego claims should be minimized depending upon the facts of the particular case. If the facts are egregious enough, and a shell corporation exists, this avenue is certainly worth pursuing. It will lead to the probable filing of a summary judgment motion by defense counsel and additional work by counsel. Therefore, the risks and benefits associated with this type of claim should be discussed with your client.

15

LITIGATING A MOTOR VEHICLE COLLISION INVOLVING A COMMERCIAL MOTOR VEHICLE FROM THE PLAINTIFF'S PERSPECTIVE

LITIGATING A TRACTOR-TRAILER case can be extremely stimulating to the trial lawyer. The same is as difficult and complex as trying a medical malpractice case. Case development, except in emergency timeframes, should be thought through with development of the case for potential industry standard violations, hiring violations, statutory and regulatory violations, and with the thought of developing a claim for punitive damages.

A. Initial Development of a Case
When you first meet with a potential tractor-trailer litigant, it is highly likely that the client will not have a broad understanding of the necessary facts for the development of your case. You must start your initial discovery through an open records request, typically called a Freedom of Information Act (FOIA) request.

You should first write to the DOT and the FMCSA to make an FOIA open records request. Their address is US Department of Transportation, 400 Seventh Street, SW, Attention: FOIA Team, Washington, DC, 20590. You need to do this in order to determine what regulatory violations have been committed by the motor carrier. The process of obtaining this information will take several months.

The second step in developing your case should be to immediately place the motor carrier on notice of the potential claim and request that they not commit any acts of spoliation of evidence. Many tractor-trailers have computer storage devices similar to black boxes in airplanes, that store data in the event of a collision. These devices will immediately be accessed by the defense attorneys and insurance companies representing the trucking company. If you do not get to this information in a prompt manner and request that the same not be destroyed, you will risk the chance of having the information deleted from the device. Once the information has been downloaded, it will be difficult, if not impossible, to obtain this information.

Your next strategic move in a tractor-trailer case will be to obtain an accident reconstruction expert to evaluate the scene. Quality reconstruction experts in commercial carrier cases are few and far between. Recent developments have allowed experts to use a laser-scanning device to recreate the entire location through laser plotting. These devices cost in excess of $100,000. The process itself is lengthy. The information can be utilized to do an actual computer reanimation that will survive an expert challenge under Daubert or Kumho Tire.

You need to perform the reconstruction immediately. Time, of course, makes the opinions of the expert subject to more challenge by opposing counsel. Days, weeks, or months can eliminate tire tracks, skid marks, and the gouge marks in the roadway. You will need to retain safety experts. You may need to retain fatigue experts and animators.

If at all possible, you should visit the accident site to make your own notes, measurements, and photographs.

Next, you need to interview prospective witnesses. Taking statements of the trucking company employees will be improbable due to instruction of defense counsel and potential ethical considerations in speaking with management from another party.

The defendant driver will most likely not speak with your detectives because of instruction from the motor carrier. The carrier will train them to refuse to speak with anyone other than law enforcement. This leaves potential investigation up to fact witnesses who may have observed the facts of the occurrence in your particular case.

This initial development stage for building a trucking case will cost $25,000 to $50,000, if done properly. The initial stage of case development will control the outcome of your case.

B. Filing Suit

The first and most important determination for the lawyer handing a tractor-trailer case is to determine whether or not to file the case in state or federal court. A sub-issue within this thought process is the determination of whether or not to file your particular case in the state where the accident happened or in the state where the trucking company is incorporated or where the driver resides. You have potential jurisdiction for the case in the state where the company is incorporated and has its principal place of business.

Cases can be filed where the driver resides. Cases may also be filed where the driver has actually been trained, hired, qualified, supervised, and/or dispatched. Many large trucking companies are regionalized with several regions in the United States. The different regions provide potential multistate jurisdiction since the motor carrier may supervise and dispatch drivers from many different regional offices, as the driver travels across the United States.

An example of jurisdiction selection is helpful. A tractor-trailer accident with a well-known national carrier occurred near Garden City. The truck driver was hired in Dallas, Texas. The truck driver was supervised by regional fleet managers in the state of Texas. He was dispatched from Dallas, Texas. The company was based outside of Kansas and Texas.

Because the defendant was an illegal alien, it was believed that a jurisdiction more favorable to Hispanics would bring out a better result for the plaintiff. The case was filed in Dallas, Texas. After substantial litigation, a ruling was obtained that Texas substantive law applied. The value of the case rose substantially once the $250,000 cap from Kansas was eliminated.

Many lawyers may choose not to seek jurisdiction in other states because of the potential cost of hiring counsel. This is a decision that must be made on a case-by-case basis, depending upon the size and merit of the particular case.

The next decision is to determine whether or not to seek federal jurisdiction. In the usual case, you will not have a federal question and must seek federal jurisdiction under Diversity of Citizenship, pursuant to 28 U.S.C. Section 1332(a).

There are many considerations to filing a case in state court versus federal court. The workload of filing a case in federal court will be significantly more time-consuming than in state court. This author, however, has found that the federal judges and magistrates are extremely fair to litigants. The benefits of filing in federal court, even though more burdensome, may be higher to the plaintiff litigant than in state court.

Obtaining federal jurisdiction in a diversity case may present a problem if you have a local driver with an out-of-state company. Procedurally, a decision can be made not to include the driver as a named party defendant to obtain complete diversity.

When drafting your petition or complaint, remember that the Federal Rules of Civil Procedure (FRCP) and Federal Rules of Evidence (FRE) have had many changes and case rulings regarding the amount of information contained in your initial petition or complaint. The general notice pleading rules of yesteryear are changing to require more thorough and exact pleadings. It is recommended that you do not use general notice pleadings and lean toward a complete and thorough development of case allegations at the start of the suit. It is better to include all potential claims from the start, rather than asking for judicial permission to add a claim. In other words, it is easier to defend a summary judgment motion than it is to convince the court that you have substantial newly discovered evidence to support a new claim through amendment.

In writing and drafting your petition or complaint, you should draft different types of allegations and different causes of action. Drafting the correct petition or complaint with the proper allegations will take significant time. You first seek redress for the plaintiff by using ordinary negligence claims. Then, you must draft the more difficult allegations by adding in most, if not all, of the following types of claims that may be applicable to your case:

1. State law ordinary negligence claims;
2. Respondeat superior claim and vicarious liability claims;
3. Hiring-related claims including negligent hiring, qualification, training, supervision, and retention;
4. Applicable regulatory violations of the FMCSR under 49 C.F.R. Sections 381-399;
5. State law violations of safety regulations pursuant to local state statutes and regulations that locally adopt the FMCSR in each state;

6. Regulatory allegations regarding the motor carrier's status;
7. Allegations that set forth the necessary foundation that the FMCSR sets forth the industry minimum standard of care to establish the violation of duties of care;
8. Allegations related to fatigue of the driver;
9. Maximum-hours violations pursuant to state and federal regulations;
10. Allegations in regard to safety protocols;
11. Punitive damage claims, including the basis for the wanton, willful, malicious, fraudulent, and reckless claims;
12. Ratification allegations that establish the motor carrier has either expressly or implied ratified the conduct of the motor carrier, its driver, and other transportation employees.

When drafting your petition or complaint, you need to consider the prospect of a claim for punitive damages. While punitive damages are difficult to obtain in many states due to statutory and case law changes regarding punitive damages, they are obtainable. While some states, like Kansas, will not allow a claim for punitive damages until an attorney has proven by clear and convincing evidence to the trial court that there is a probability of success on the punitive damage claims at trial, there are ways to avoid these types of procedural rules and limits by filing cases in federal court under Diversity of Citizenship due to the fact that federal courts do not usually follow state procedural rules. In Kansas, a plaintiff may seek a claim for punitive damages under Federal Diversity cases based upon the case of *Oleson v. K-Mart*, 185 F.R.D. 631 (D. Kan. 1999). The state procedural rule is avoided in Federal Diversity cases.

The punitive damage consideration of the case will be based upon either wanton, willful, or malicious behavior of the truck driver and trucking company. Many states require a showing of reckless disregard or indifference to human suffering or gross negligence, instead of these more specific types of conduct. This will most normally be in regard to the trucking company forcing its drivers to violate maximum hours-of-service rules of the FMCSR and/or the truck driver driving in a fatigued state to comply with motor carrier delivery scheduling. Many truck drivers are forced to exceed the maximum hours-of-service rules to meet mandatory on-time delivery schedules.

C. Discovery

Winning your case is contingent upon obtaining useful discovery. Many defense lawyers will construe the written discovery strictly, thereby leading to a need for motions to compel. The necessary information sought cannot always be obtained prior to a deposition being taken. In most cases, if you do not get your initial discovery responded to properly, then immediate deposition of the appropriate business management personnel will be necessary.

In some cases, it may be justifiable to actually take a deposition prior to submission of written discovery. This is because many times a witness will answer a question under oath and divulge information which otherwise would not be obtainable by written discovery without motions to compel.

Any discovery sought should include requests for safety audits. Safety audits and reviews contain extremely useful information against the trucking company. The safety audits and reviews are based upon insurance company evaluation of the safety practices of the trucking company. Safety audits and reviews don't always contain the words "safety review" or "safety audit." Defense counsel may fail to identify a document that is a "safety review" or "safety audit" document because it is named inappropriately in the discovery request. Safety audits and reviews evaluate the safety practices of the trucking company and then make safety recommendations and/or requirements for a change of the company practices. Many motor carriers will ignore the recommendations and/or requirements of the safety auditor. Discovery of these audits will provide a significant base of evidence to establish negligence and to make a claim for punitive damages. Insurance carriers must undergo mandatory safety audits to determine their safety compliance history with the FMCSR. The insurance company will send in an in-house or independent contractor to study and evaluate the past safety practices of the company and the total number of preventable and non-preventable accidents. Once the number is too high, the trucking company will have difficulty obtaining liability insurance. This leads to many trucking companies taking a self-insured retention for the first $250,000 or $500,000 of liability where the company is required to settle their own claims. They have an insurance carrier, but the coverage does not come into play until they reach a certain level of damages to property or bodily injury and personal injury to human beings injured in an accident.

In many cases, the deposition testimony of a manager of the company will lead to evidence that a safety audit or review exists and will confirm whether the same is maintained in the course of business. Discovery of safety audits is one of the most useful evidentiary tools available in litigating a trucking case.

Discovery by depositions should be obtained from the following management personnel:

1. Safety director at lower level and vice president of safety
2. Risk management director

3. Fleet manager
4. Operations manager
5. Dispatch personnel
6. Hiring manager and training manager
7. Citation department personnel who regularly check the motor vehicle record history for each driver in the motor carrier's fleet
8. Disciplinary persons in human resources
9. Road test personnel
10. Maintenance personnel
11. President and CEO

Another area of discovery that needs to be discussed is the company's dealings with regulatory agencies such as the USDOT and with state regulatory agencies like the local state DOT. Interrogatories and Requests for Production of Documents may be narrowly and strictly construed by defense counsel, leading to a poor result in discovery. The discovery requests need to be specifically crafted to lead to non-objectionable evidence.

Interrogatories and Requests for Production of Documents need to be drafted specifically to obtain information regarding the following:

1. Trip and operational documents
2. Hours-of-service records
3. Maintenance files and records
4. Policy procedure manuals used to hire, qualify, supervise, and train drivers
5. Copies of citations or violations a company has had for violation of state and federal laws relating to the FMCSR
6. Copies of insurance company audits, safety reviews, safety studies, and other evaluations on the company
7. Instructional and training materials for all drivers

8. Citation department records for all trucks the company runs in its fleet
9. Trip expense information for the driver and the particular case being litigated
10. Cargo pickup and delivery documents
11. Bills of lading and/or cargo manifest documents
12. Dispatch and operational records
13. Call-in records
14. Trip check-in or financial settlement sheets
15. Safety audits
16. Disciplinary records on the driver
17. Copies of all accident records for the driver and co-drivers, including minor property damage incidents

D. Trial

The trial of your case must be meticulously planned and implemented. Pretrial motions, including motions in limine and Daubert/Kumho Tire motions, will define the scope of your trial.

One of the most important considerations for the trial of your case will be the preparation of your jury instructions. Jury instructions will help convince the jury of what law or regulation has been violated. You should seek jury instructions on each and every violation of ordinary negligence that applies, but more importantly, you should seek jury instructions on all FMCSA regulations that have been violated. The jury instructions sought should be prepared prior to the commencement of trial.

Review and critique all deposition testimony. Video-deposition testimony is far more useful than a written transcript. During discovery, if you can obtain an admission against interest or an acknowledgment by a company manager that the truck driver has violated some safety rule of either the FMCSR or a safety protocol of the company, then this particular type of evidence can be played before the jury during examination of the witness and again in closing arguments. Many trials are won or lost over a few words of a managerial witness admitting some safety violation of the company or its driver.

The analysis of the company's own safety manuals, protocols, training documents, and employee reviews is critical to winning your case. A thorough study should be made of the company's own safety-related documents so that demonstrative exhibits can be made of all incriminating safety evidence.

Voir dire must be drafted to inquire into the mind and heart of each and every prospective juror to determine their thoughts, philosophies, and self-learned teachings in regard to safety practices. Every attorney performing the jury selection process should inquire of jurors individually and not by panel questions. Many legal seminars teach attorneys to ask general panel questions with a showing of hands for all jurors in regard to a particular question. The inherent problem with questioning in this manner is that people in a group and will often refrain from voicing their opinion to a given question. Thus, it is absolutely necessary that you question each and every juror for a moment of time independently of all other jurors on a particular subject. For example, you may ask an open-ended question about whether or not the jurors have a particular thought against awarding pain and suffering. The usual panel response will be a lack of response from all jurors. Upon individual questioning, it is highly likely that you will find many strong personal opinions by individual jurors. While Mr. Jones may fail to respond to an open-ended panel question about his thoughts about pain and suffering, upon further individual questioning he may inform you that he has a personal philosophy and thought process that would prevent him from awarding pain and suffering.

Reptile-type questions should be used following the recent trend in plaintiffs' lawyers attempting to understand the reptilian mind of the average juror. Books and seminars are available to plaintiffs' attorneys to learn how to fight back on the insurance industry's lobbying and advertising efforts attempting to convince potential jurors that fraudulent cases are being brought by plaintiffs. This intense effort by the insurance industry started in the nineties and has continued to build, which gives the average jury a skewed view of injury victims. It is clear that jurors no longer care about pain and suffering. Jurors think in terms of compensating injury victims for damages related to abandonment, humiliation, loss of mobility, or the ability to ambulate, and other more important factors related to substantial losses in a person's change of life pattern after or during the accident recovery period.

To obtain a proper perspective of each juror, you must talk to him or her individually and openly. You need to inquire about all of their biases and prejudices because people do not admit that they are biased or prejudiced until you reach a nerve through a specific question to that particular juror. Your case and its final outcome will hinge upon your ability to select the appropriate jurors for your case.

The overall process of trying a trucking case will be lengthy and involved. Of necessity, you will be required to show evidence of the regulatory violations. The first several days of trial will be devoted to proving liability and establishing violations of the regulatory framework of the FMCSR. It will require the use of experts to inform the jury how the particular regulations have been violated. Defense counsel will retain experts who will testify that the regulations have been complied with, while Plaintiff's counsel will testify how the regulations have been violated.

Experts in the trucking industry are in great demand by both sides and are extremely costly to both sides in the litigation process. Both sides may choose to utilize accident reconstruction experts, plus a safety expert and/or regulatory expert. The cost of putting these experts on can be overwhelming to the average lawyer. In a proper case, you should be prepared to spend at least $50,000 to try your case from start to finish. The cost could easily exceed $100,000 if done appropriately.

While many lawyers disagree on whether the opening or closing is the most important aspect of the case, it is quite certain that jurors remember the first and last things they hear. This does not mean that they do not listen to and focus on evidence in between, but psychological studies indicate that people retain the very first thought that they are presented, and they will remember information more readily if they have a visual cue with the presentation of the evidence. Visual evidence is remembered at a much greater rate than auditory evidence. Thus, the lawyer will want to prepare both the visual and auditory presentation prior to commencement of trial so that their combined effect is realized before presentation. Studies of jury pools by psychologists have led to an understanding of the mechanism of the jury's understanding of evidence. It is important to understand that a combination of visual cue evidence must be combined with auditory evidence because of the innate differences in how jurors perceive and react to the presentation of evidence. Some jurors may see evidence and remember little of it, while others who received an auditory cue remember the crucial part of the case.

Your closing argument will result in the culmination of your efforts. Remember that evidence in your case may be overwhelming due to its size and complexity. Find the most important evidence. Magnify and explain it for the jury. Utilize your discovery to convince the jury you have been honest and forthright in the presentation of your case. Use your discovery to show them why you should win. If you have been successful in obtaining a managerial admission against interest, plan it in closing for the jury.

As a final thought, address each and every fact for and against your client. Failure to address a relevant fact could cause you to lose your entire case. One caveat to this rule is to not be led astray by opposing counsel's case. Argue your position with zealous candor. Be certain you are right and your conviction will be heard.

REFERENCES

http://www.businessinsider.com/trucking-industry-infographic-2013-4

http://en.wikipedia.org/wiki/Trucking_industry_in_the_United_States

http://csa.fmcsa.dot.gov

http://www.fmcsa.dot.gov

http://www.fmcsa.gov/regulations

http://www-nrd.nhtsa.dot.gov/Pubs/809-569.pdf

http://www.nhtsa.gov/NCSA

http://www.rita.dot.gov/bts/

http://www.fhwa.dot.gov/policy/r2.htm

http://www.rita.dot.gov/bts/sites/rita.dot.gov.bts/files/subject_areas/international/index.html

http://www.fmcsa.dot.gov/regulations/hours-of-service

http://www.fmcsa.dot.gov/regulations/cargo-securement/cargo-securement-rules

http://www.fmcsa.dot.gov/regulations/cargo-securement/drivers-handbook-cargo-securement-introduction

http://www.freightmobility.com/TruckStats.html

http://www.trucking.org/News_and_Information_Reports_Industry_Data.aspx

http://factfinder2.census.gov/faces/tableservices/jsf/pages/productview.xhtml?pid=CFS_2012_00P1&prodType=table

http://www.truckline.com/Trucking_Issues_Highway_
Infrastructure.aspx
http://factfinder2.census.gov/faces/tableservices/jsf/pages/
productview.xhtml?pid=CFS_2012_00P2&prodType=table
http://factfinder2.census.gov/bkmk/navigation/1.0/
en/d_dataset:CFS_2012/d_business_economic_
series:PRELIMINARY_STATISTICS
http://www.iihs.org/iihs/topics/t/large-trucks/fatalityfacts/
large-trucks
http://www.hg.org/trucking-accidents.html
http://www.transport.govt.nz/assets/Uploads/Research/
Documents/Trucks-crashfacts-2013.pdf
http://www.fhwa.dot.gov/publications/research/safety/
humanfac/04085/index.cfm#top
http://www.nationalowneroperatorjobs.com/truck-
driving-accidents.html
http://www.statista.com/statistics/195100/averageoperating-
truck-speed-on-selected-us-interstate-highways/
http://www.fourwheeler.com/how-to/0607
or-toyota-pickup-truck-buyers-guide/
http://www.gti-logistics.com/en/useful/trucks
http://www.specguideonline.com/search/articulated-trucks
http://cta.ornl.gov/vtmarketreport/pdf/chapter3_heavy_
trucks.pdf
http://www.guinnessworldrecords.com/world-
records/1/highest-vehicle-mileage
http://www.advisorperspectives.com/dshort/updates/DOT-
Miles-Driven.php
http://www.truckinfo.net/trucking/stats.htm#
Accident%20Stats
http://www.truckaccidentresourcecenter.com/
truck-accident-statistics/
http://www.nationalowneroperatorjobs.com/truck-driving-
accidents.html

http://www.truckingtruth.com/Articles/Trucking-Industry-Articles/trucking_johnson.html

http://www.hg.org/article.asp?id=29623

http://www.volvotrucks.com/SiteCollection Documents/VTC/Corporate/Values/ART%20Report%20 2013_150dpi.pdf

http://www.kaltire.com/commercial/truck/tire-wear-conditions/

http://psycnet.apa.org/books/10107/011

http://proxy.baremetal.com/csdp.org/research/jed20085.pdf

http://unsafetrucks.org/common_causes_truck_accidents/

http://injury.findlaw.com/car-accidents/common-causes-of-commercial-truck-accidents.html

http://www.commdiginews.com/business-2/texting-while-driving-a-leading-cause-of-auto-accidents-death-among-teen-drivers-12781/

http://www.mayoclinic.org/diseases-conditions/depression/in-depth/antidepressants/art-any   system killed 20046273

http://www.cb39.org/csa_fatigued_driving_violation_severity.html

http://www.huffingtonpost.com/2014/02/03/truck-driver-regulations-_n_4704195.html

http://ntl.bts.gov/lib/51000/51400/51417/Efficacy-of-HOS-Restart-Rule-Report.pdf

http://www.newsday.com/news/nation/study-texting-while-driving-now-leading-cause-of-death-for-teen-drivers-1.5226036

http://www.distraction.gov/content/get-the-facts/facts-and-statistics.html

http://www.jhsph.edu/research/centers-and-institutes/mid-atlantic-public-health-training-center/_documents/032013_Distracted_driving_Swedler.pdf

http://www.dnainfo.com/new-york/20131203/spuyten-duyvil/metro-north-train-driver-dozed-off-before-crash-sources-say

http://www.distraction.gov/download/research-pdf/comparison-of-cellphone-driver-drunk-driver.pdf

http://apps.dmv.ca.gov/pubs/hdbk/shr_lgtruck_rv.htm

http://www.udot.utah.gov/trucksmart/dld/Truck_Smart_No_Zone_Fact_Sheet.pdf

http://www.cga.ct.gov/2004/rpt/2004-r-0838.htm

http://www.truckingtruth.com/trucking_blogs/Article-1346/a-truckers-day-of-bad-weather

http://www.bls.gov/ooh/transportation-and-material-moving/heavy-and-tractor-trailer-truck-drivers.htm

http://www.truck-drivers-money-saving-tips.com/falsifying.html

http://www.thenewamerican.com/world-news/europe/item/16477-eu-exploring-scheme-to-nstall-speed-limiting-devices-on-cars

http://www.rms.nsw.gov.au/usingroads/penalties/speeding.html

http://www.legalinfo.com/content/truck-accidents/truck-accident-statistics.html

http://www.thetruckersreport.com/feds-raid-trucking-company-for-forcing-drivers-to-falsify-logbooks/

http://axenty.com/blog/ask/digital-logbooks-and-the-faa/

http://www.hg.org/trucking-accidents.html

https://www.tdlr.texas.gov/towing/towrules.htm

http://info.sos.state.tx.us/pls/pub/readtac$ext.TacPage?sl=R&app=9&p_dir=&p_rloc=&p_tloc=&p_ploc=&pg=1&p_tac=&ti=16&pt=4&ch=86&rl=400

www.ingramcontent.com/pod-product-compliance
Lightning Source LLC
Chambersburg PA
CBHW020906180526
45163CB00007B/2642